For Mother

Negativities
The Limits of Life

Joseph Margolis

Temple University

Charles E. Merrill Publishing Company
A Bell & Howell Company
Columbus, Ohio 43216

Published by
Charles E. Merrill Publishing Company
A Bell & Howell Company
Columbus, Ohio 43216

ISBN: 0-675-08732-5 paperbound
0-675-08729-5 clothbound

Library of Congress Catalog Card Number: 74-22913

1 2 3 4 5 6 7 8 9—81 80 79 78 77 76 75

The following chapters have appeared in other publications and have been revised for inclusion in this book:

Chapter 3, "Abortion": *Ethics* 84 (1973): 51-61. Copyright 1973 by the University of Chicago Press.

Chapter 4, "War": as "War and Ideology," in *Philosophy, Morality, and International Affairs,* ed. Virginia Held, Sidney Morgenbesser, and Thomas Nagel (New York: Oxford University Press, 1974).

Chapter 6, "Punishment": *Social Theory and Practice* 2 (1973): 347-63.

Printed in the United States of America

Preface

I have written these essays out of necessity. A good deal of contemporary philosophy focused on questions of public policy invites us to believe that the analysis of fundamental concepts somehow yields instruction about the rights and wrongs of personal conduct. I have never believed it, but instead have always believed that philosophy must give way to ideology where commitment is concerned. Still, my previous work failed to include a sustained effort to show how to analyze the principal categories bearing on conduct in a way that remained informed and professionally rigorous as well as responsive to the need we all have to take a stand on the deepest problems of life. I had not appreciated the gap partly because I had actually written a little on illness and health and partly because an earlier fashion in moral philosophy encouraged a certain avoidance of the gut issues. That is all changed now. On the other hand, once I was reasonably clear about what topics could not be avoided, I was really quite shocked to find how little attention philosophy has paid them. Here and there, a piece appears on death or war or abortion. But by and large, given the insistence on "relevance," it is most instructive to see how very little has actually been done.

What I have tried to do here is to show both how remarkably systematic are our informal views of an entire array of categories —what I have called negativities, for want of a better term—and how a philosophical analysis of each decisively bears on whatever doctrinal commitments we may make, without dictating the "correct" commitment. I was myself surprised to discover these interconnections. I believed they were there but could not articulate them until I had actually worked through a fair portion of the current literature. That in itself was a pleasant discovery. In fact, I have tried to read the most informed accounts bearing on each topic, which happen to be both non-philosophical and professional in their own right. As far as I know, there is no unified philosophical discussion of the range of topics here collected, certainly none that is current and reasonably widely informed.

But the necessity I felt comes from another source as well. I find that my professional efforts have gradually converged on the distinction of the human person and that even what seemed most remote and unrelated has proved to bear, sometimes intimately, on the clarification of that issue. The largest clues I have found are these: that persons are culturally emergent entities and that persons are physically embodied. I hope to be able to offer a theory of persons on another occasion, but in the present context I find myself dialectically constrained to consider the compatibility of my account of insanity, perversion, crime, and the rest, with these essential clues. The upshot, which I hope will seem both fresh and instructive, is that there are no natural norms by which to guide ourselves in managing the moral and political problems generated by each topic *and* that there need not be any in order to make rationally informed commitments. Here, I rely very heavily on whatever may be the prevalent interests of any human society, without presuming to say what it ought to concern itself with. The idea of philosophers giving such direction, *pace* Plato, has always seemed to me quite laughable. In any case, conceding my own foolishness and the foolishness of my colleagues, it would be dreadfully depressing to think that the solution of the most important problems really depended on the leadership of philosophers. Philosophy, as I see it, concerns itself with the coherence and rationality of any analysis, proposal, commitment, or the like that we might make, but the instinct for developing viable policies that large portions of the human race might be willing to support lies elsewhere.

I do honestly believe that our most strenuous efforts to study problems objectively fall victim, in the most subtle ways, to antecedent loyalties. No one is exempt. Consequently, no one can provide a final answer to the puzzles raised by the negativities considered. The work goes on in that self-corrective way that only entire societies can sustain. Nevertheless, I hope that the distinction of what follows lies in its exhibiting a way of handling issues that come as close as they possibly can to the entire span of human life, without betraying the nerve of philosophy. I have called this effort, simply to stress how deliberate it is, the study of rational minima. My notion here is that the best philosophy can do is to sort out those conceptual constraints that every viable policy or doctrine of the relevant kind must accommodate in order to be rationally responsible in gathering our loyalties, in action. Ideology, as I have suggested, captures our animal vitality; philosophy presses to make it as coherent as possible. In any case, I am persuaded that it is time we ceased pretending that we *know* the correct way to arrange the life of man.

The strategy of the book embodies, I should like to believe, a larger theory about moral discourse that completely undercuts the traditional opposition between so-called cognitivist and noncognitivist theories. I think it impossible to discover the sufficient norms for the moral justification of any significant range of conduct (which suggests noncognitivism); but I think it quite possible to formulate some of the necessary qualifications, either formal or conditional or dialectical, that any rationally defended moral justification would have to meet (which suggests cognitivism). Furthermore, though I concede that moral judgments may, given a relevant set of rules and criteria, be said to be true or false (which suggests cognitivism), I insist that the validity of no substantive moral norms depends on the exercise of distinctly moral faculties and that the validity of no set of norms sufficient to justify conduct can be confirmed (which suggests noncognitivism). In short, I hold that given conduct and given judgments may be indefensible on entirely nontendentious grounds, but that they cannot be fully confirmed nontendentiously. In this sense, philosophy gives way to ideology. I know of no sustained theory of this sort in the current literature.

I must give a word of special thanks to Grace Stuart, who has helped me once again to put my work in readable form; to my friends of the Ossabaw Island Project, who arranged for the leisure to complete the editing; and to colleagues who have tested portions of the manuscript. Also, I should note that several chapters owe much to previously published drafts on particular topics.

Contents

Introduction

Human beings have always sought to fix their essential nature: man is said to be the political animal or the animal that lives in cities, the rational animal, the self-conscious animal, the sapient or artisan or laughing species, the symbolizing animal, the creature that has mastered speech, the violent animal, the animal that wars against its own breed, the being with a tragic sense or the being between beasts and angels, the alien or alienated creature, and, finally, the creature that lacks a nature. Furthermore, being what he is, man is enjoined to follow his nature: to seek happiness or pleasure or equilibrium, to fulfill his duty or station or interests, to obey the law of nature, to transvalue his values, to actualize himself or to become his true self, to be authentic, to act in accord with reason, to work out his salvation, to accept necessity, to be free, to give laws to himself, to promote the well-being of humanity, to cultivate his own garden. There is no need, therefore, to add to the definition of man or to the recipes of life. That is all behind us, in a huge "wisdom literature" that has spawned all the great

1

movements and quarrels of human history. Its power, clothed as religion, politics, economics, art, morality, law, medicine, science, education, or philosophy, is unmistakable. There is no reason to think that it will abate or that newer instructions about man's nature and function will not continue to attract the devotion of large societies. However, though we have collected the competing lessons of that literature, we still do not know how to confirm the definitions and recipes of human life without serving merely as the partisans of one view or another.

We know that man is not merely a distinctive animal; whatever is most characteristic of his cultural achievement (in fact, the very achievement of a diverse and historically changing culture) depends on some special employment of his animal endowment. Feral children appear incapable of mastering speech and human culture, though they can be somewhat domesticated; and language itself seems, on the most recent evidence, not altogether inaccessible to other primates. We also know that the full development of the cerebral cortex undoubtedly postdates the somewhat cultural life of the upright hominids, hunters and warriors in a spare landscape—weapon making, organized along new lines, exposed on the hostile surface of the earth once and for all. Not only has the survival of emergent man been conditional on the development of a rudimentary culture but his most distinctive physical endowment, his brain, has apparently accommodated that culture and permitted a *further* development of it. In this sense, in the sense in which human communities have never existed without an articulated language and culture, never without cultural norms and values in terms of which to organize themselves, to relate to other peoples, to exploit the resources of the planet, *man has no assignable place in nature by reference to which his cultural objectives may be straightforwardly appraised.* In other words, man has no normative nature; what we find are only the actual norms and recipes of life that particular human cultures have managed to invent. Consequently, the confirmation of one set of values as superior to all others is nothing but the loyalty of one set of partisans pitted against the loyalty of another.

This single fact has extraordinary implications. For instance, our concern with planetary ecology is hopelessly mismanaged to the extent that it insists that man restore "the balance of nature." There is no natural order to which man can *return;* his distinctive mode of life has always been to exploit the natural resources of the planet and to create an environment conformable with whatever values his various and changing cultures have generated. This is not to say, of course, that ecology makes no sense, only that the question it poses is not one of restoring man to his natural place, or even restoring a natural order without considering man at all, but a question of deciding what human programs physical nature can support (with what losses) and what changes in human objectives are culturally viable. Similarly, even physical medicine cannot ignore the cultural dimension of health. Those conditions classified as illness and disease vary, in principle, with our cultural objectives. A substantial change in technology, ideology, or environment (all subject to cultural manipulation) affects our realistic expectations about the body's ability to perform, *a fortiori*, such changes affect the norms of mental health. In fact, medicine is a key discipline in this respect, since it may be the only indispensable profession claiming the status of an ideologically neutral science and committed, at the same time, to normative values that seem incapable of such neutrality. So, if the ecological concept of waste and the medical concept of illness are inextricably dependent on the dominant values of a given culture, such infra-societal concepts as crime and punishment could not possibly escape being dependent in the same way. Here, then, we see something of the global import of admitting that human beings, however they may be embodied in a biologically gifted stock, are, uniquely, culturally emergent beings. Whatever the key to human nature may be, it must lie in the nature of culture itself.

The thesis is radical. Human beings have a nature, in the neutral sense that we are certainly able to formulate a great many truths about them. But they lack a nature if, by "nature," we mean some essential state, whose detection correctly informs us of the "proper" or "true" or "natural" use of human life itself. Men, of course, have always shown the most extraordinary tendency to believe that God or earthly science has already managed to confirm whatever "natural" norms we are prepared to commit ourselves to.

Nevertheless, it should not be thought that this admission entirely subverts the prospect of reasonable instructions for the use of human life. For one thing, privileged claims about natural and revealed norms are responsible for every historically prominent instance of man's inhumanity to man. How, then, could exposing their indefensibility add anything more to the world's distress? Religious, political, and economic wars are much too much alike, and technology has already shown us the meaning of total disaster. Perhaps a new skepticism about absolute or natural values may even temper our destructive tendencies. It is hard to believe that it could fire them any more. Second, both formal and dialectical constraints bear on the consistency, coherence, scope, believability, relevance, generality, viability, and non-arbitrariness of any and all normative proposals, restricting their rational eligibility without yet committing us to any particular doctrine. Not that men are able to do without an ideology or creed. But in order to avoid mere partisanship, to make our loyalties as rational as possible, we must fall back to the central experiences of men, those ubiquitous and unforgettable crises, challenges, and confrontations that test the mettle of every promising ideology. Thus seen, the world's greatest and most compelling doctrines must be elaborations at least, along selected lines of commitment, of certain minimal truths. If not, there is no guidance at all to be recommended.

It seems that certain negative conditions of life are the most instructive in this regard. Death and illness must be the most fundamental, since they are shared with the animate world at large. Indeed, every culture appears to institutionalize distinctly human "negativities," the basic forms of losing and limiting life: suicide, crime, deviance, insanity, inequality, alienation, and waste, as well as such distinctly negative correctives as anarchy, punishment, war, revolution, abortion, euthanasia, and genocide. It helps to bring these concepts together, because one hardly realizes otherwise how very much the world's ideologies are focused on the negative conditions of human life and how systematically they are related to one another.

The substantive analysis of the negativities selected remains to be provided. But we need to be clear about the strategy of the inquiry at the start. Certain tangential arguments cannot be conveniently supplied here—for instance, a detailed account of the relationship between human animals and human persons. A certain physical endowment distinguishes the first, particularly, sentience and a complex brain; and a certain cultural achievement distinguishes the second, particularly, the power of speech and self-reference. To contrast the two is not to encourage a dualism of mind and body (or to show how to avoid it); it is to stress only that men alone reflect on the point of their existence and, doing so, invent a variety of rationalizations for pursuing life and a variety for ending and restricting it. Man discovers that he is a creature of culture, that his animal resources cannot direct him to his proper cultural objectives; he also finds that the creeds to which he gives his allegiance are in turn cultural inventions provided under the same conditions under which he was groomed to be the creature he has become. In terms of the survival of the race, these remarks may be irrelevancies: obviously there has never been a dearth of doctrine to fascinate and compel. But on any fair view, our earthly creeds hardly converge, in the sense that every set of favored values is under fire from the vantage of other equally compelling convictions and none is beyond dispute or the danger of losing its animal attraction.

We are well advised, then, to try to isolate the themes of human life that shape whatever creeds and ideologies compel us. We do this in order to understand whatever minimal truths there may be that every viable doctrine must exploit. The truths in question are thought to be non-partisan; their exploitation cannot be. Still, how can we pretend to step back from our lives to survey, neutrally, whatever persuades us to live as we do? Objectivity, one hopes, is not altogether impossible. No one can escape the attraction of his own orientation; but the inquiry is dialectical and depends on the confronting discoveries of the race. In effect, we pool our intelligence, exposing one by one every presumption, forcing ourselves, against ourselves, to concede whatever is unconfirmed and unconfirmable, sorting out the least doubtful and least tendentious implications of human life.

Our strategy is designed, then, not to provide the most convincing normative values but only the most convincing array of non-normative truths that any rationally attractive ideology would be bound to accommodate. Commitment to a normative doctrine cannot be merely rational, that is, based entirely on compelling reasons, if, as has been said, there are no viable means for confirming, among competing norms, the natural or correct ones. Ideologies are not, for that reason, irrational; we sustain our lives by our orderly convictions. Rationally, we appraise the coherence and defensibility of whatever doctrines compel us, but their attraction is ultimately linked to the animal power of life itself.

No matter how varied our doctrines may be, any survey of what the race has most seriously concerned itself with in its typical commitments would have to admit at least three ineliminable conditions of animal endowment: death, illness, and the inequality of physical gifts and abilities. Death, of course, drives men to invent the most extravagant denials. The question we ask ourselves, therefore, is precisely what can be said about the nature of death that is pointedly and universally true, in order to draw out those considerations the disregard of which is impossible for any claim that holds our rational allegiance as fully informed agents. We scan what we know of ourselves in order to temper every relevant commitment, to isolate the gaps in whatever arguments support our favored ideologies.

Our insight tends to be largely formal or dialectical. For instance, if we approve of or condemn suicide, we are bound to show how some overriding rule regarding man's use of his own life is satisfied or violated. The question naturally follows a general account of death and the implications of man's cultural existence. Again, if we approve of or condemn war we must show how we may pass from talking about the responsibilities of individual men to those of collective entities, since war is ascribable only to entities like nations. So, beginning with death as the limit of animal life, we pursue those cultural elements that fix most clearly our efforts to deal with our own mortality: for instance, suicide, where one takes one's own life; murder, where another's life is taken; war, where killing is justified or condemned in collective terms; abortion, where the lives of future persons are taken; illness, where the decline of animal vitality is confronted; punishment, where the use of one's powers is restricted by way of forfeit.

Even death and illness, of course, are culturally qualified, since man alone reflects on their inevitability. The only other negative condition of comparable importance that appears in both natural and cultural forms is that of unequal gifts and opportunities. As death is the chief concern of religion, inequality, especially the inequality of power, is the chief concern of politics. And as religion has generated the most extravagant theories by which to reconcile us to mortality, political speculation has attempted, with equal extravagance, to justify existing inequalities or to correct them. War, revolution, anarchy, and some of what we call crime (as a sort of infra-political analogue) are the principal negative processes by which the unequal distribution of power and material goods is extended and reduced. Inequality is of interest, also, in being at least partially dependent on animal endowment. Here, racial differences and differences in intelligence, health, and sexual orientation have occupied us most. Both the racial matter and the question of sexual deviance are particularly decisive, because, in effect, they force us to consider once again whether there are natural norms to which we must conform: sexual deviance tests the limits of tolerance regarding admissible human conduct; and racial differences suggest the justification for generalizing in pointedly normative ways about specified sub-groups of the human race. The matter of insanity should be mentioned as well, since it bridges the puzzles of health and deviance.

There is, also, the analogue of death for the environment at large: waste, the exhaustion of the world's resources. Relative to illness, we think of waste as pollution; relative to political life, as the by-product of inequality; relative to the provision of an exploitable world for future generations, as injustice. Finally, grasping the double finitude of death and waste, the exhaustion of one's own life and one's world, men confront a further negativity—alienation—which, most succinctly, concerns the very distinction of human nature, the isolating power of man's inherent inability to find in the physical world any adequate norms for the direction of his cultural existence. Alienation, therefore, is simply the generic form of all the conditions mentioned.

These, then, may be termed the principal negativities of human life. They have interlocking implications not only because of the conceptual linkages sketched but because of the dependence of their analysis on our underlying theory of what it is to be a human person. The fact that man is essentially a cultural creature is the decisive consideration. It is, however, not a fact that can be established in any simple observational way though it relies on and collects all relevant observational data. There are excellent reasons, also, for supposing that to admit animal species as natural species is hardly sufficient to provide for "natural" human norms. For one thing, the human race is sufficiently different from every other animal that the interests of any other stock have very little to do with the most distinctively human endeavors. For another, it is impossible to provide norms for any of the other animal species. What is the natural function of the baboon or the fruit fly or the whale or the starfish? Speculating thus, we anthropomorphize the life of the various species, reading back into the animal world what we have already specified for the human; in fact, there hardly seems to be, among animals, any systematic way of distinguishing "personal" and breed values, where the sole scale along which appraisal makes any clear sense at all is that of survival.

We concede, of course, analogous prudential interests on the part of human beings, for instance, survival, reduction of pain, gratification of desire, security, sustained bodily functioning, stable social environment, and the like. Conceding these, we admit behavior congruent with such objectives to be *prima facie* rational, in the relatively innocent and provisional sense that no human culture could actually survive without some sustained attention to them. Departures of at least two sorts may yet be rational: for one, individuals and aggregates may prefer values that override these provisional ones, without a loss of rationality, as in suicide and personal sacrifice; for another, entire societies may subordinate their present use of whatever satisfies their prudential interests, in the name of values catering to the interests of future generations, as in war and conservation. Hence, prudential values are provisional, statistically confirmed, no more than a concession to what every viable ideology requires; also, such values are determinable rather than determinate, enabling values only, subject to higher considerations varying from context to context.

The analysis of the negativities mentioned, therefore, explains how prudential interests are determinately adjusted by every creed that supplies us with overriding values. In that sense, it confirms the importance of our undertaking and the prospect of achieving our objective: to isolate the most fundamental implications of the nature of human life that no ideology can ignore and from which no ideology could be straightforwardly derived.

1

Death

Unless privileged articles of faith are invoked, we are all moved by death essentially in accord with the view of Epicurus: "When we are, death is not; and when death is, we are not." Dying is living in a specially diminished way, but death is not a process or an act: it is the limit of life. We ask what its significance is simply because our animal vitality is manifested in what we are pleased to call the significance of life: our devotion to the one obliges us to ask whether there is some continuity of purpose involving the other, and perhaps what lies beyond the other. It is psychologically disruptive to have been persuaded that there *is* a point to living, and then merely and in a bland way to be unpuzzled by the ubiquity of death. Projects undertaken are cut short too soon, allegiances are wasted, promises are left unfulfilled, and all hopes and fears are affected by an apparently senseless factor.

Some have held that one cannot imagine or conceive his own death. Goethe and Freud apparently held such a view—Goethe, in fact, so enthusiastically that he was persuaded that he would not die.[1] It is hopeless to gain immortality on the strength of a poor argument and it

is demonstrable that the alleged inconceivability rests on an equivocation. Two considerations are decisive. First, we must distinguish between the conceiving agent and the content of his conception. Thus I
may easily conceive of situations that do not involve me, as far as the
content of my conception is concerned; I may, for instance, conceive of
an early state of the earth in which there was no life at all, not even
mine. Second, we must not suppose that in *my* conceiving a state of
affairs that excludes my existence, I am conceiving of myself both
present and absent, both existing and not existing, that is,
contradictorily.

When I conceive of a period of the world before my birth, I am not
conceiving of a period in which I am somehow present, unborn, as if
present and actual life stretched in an inexplicable way to include my
birth and the gap before I was born; and when I conceive of a period
after my death, I am not conceiving of a period in which I am somehow
present, though dead, as if my life stretched in an inexplicable way to
include my death and the gap following my death.[2] To conceive of
one's birth or death is to conceive of an interval in which one begins to
exist in a world that does not yet include one's life or to conceive of an
interval in which some state of affairs obtains in which one's life is no
longer included.

The conceivability of one's own death needs to be stressed because
the capacity entailed is thought to distinguish man from every other
living creature. All creatures are mortal but, apparently, only man
grasps his own mortality and finitude. The theme is the focus of
existentialist theories of human nature.[3] The ulterior question, of
course, concerns the significance of death. But since it has been alleged
that it is self-contradictory to hold that one can conceive his own death,
we have had to dispose of a false argument threatening the very
coherence of our question. Surely it is counterintuitive to deny that the
man who asks his physician whether he will soon die is asking a
perfectly intelligible question. The truth is that the matter has been
confused with more quarrelsome questions, for instance, with that of
whether a man can conceive or dream of *his* observing his own death or
funeral.

But death is only an extreme instance of a family of conditions that
invite the same speculation. For instance, a man may be in an irreversible coma for an interval in which he continues to "live" only if
nourished by the deliberate efforts of other human beings. To mention
the possibility is to draw attention to a normative use of the verb "live"
that we favor: men are said to live not only when the minimal metabolic
processes of biological survival obtain but also when they are *capable*,

so surviving, of pursuing any of an indefinitely wide variety of pur-
poseful ways of life that conform, as non-tendentiously as we please,
to the norms of *rational, civilized,* or *personal* life. Hence we say, "that's
no life," "he's as good as dead," "he's no more than a vegetable,"
"that's a living death." The point is that, even admitting the intelligibil-
ity of one's own death, it is difficult to talk about the significance of
death *simpliciter:* irresistibly, speculation takes the form of thinking
about the permanent and irreversible *deprivation* of doctrinally favored
values of life or about the significance of one's life summed up. On the
condition that we have not yet succeeded in confirming the "true"
values of life, and on the condition that it may well be impossible to do
so, we may fairly take it that such speculation is inherently partisan.

Death is an evil because and only because *we* suppose we lose
thereby some *prospectively* favored condition or opportunity; actual
death is neither good nor evil. The counterpart for those who deny
death or construe it as a temporary discontinuity is that the favored
state is still accessible and that, after apparent death, *we* may be ranked
and graded with respect to it. Both views fail to come to terms with
Epicurus' maxim: to admit death in the relevant sense is to preclude
ascriptions to continuing persons.

In death, there is no sense in which *you* can still be deprived of this or
that opportunity; or, in which *you* can still aspire or lose hope, whether
in Hell or at some point in the cycle of karma. To speak of the interests
of the dead, for instance, as formulated in a will, is to speak of constraints on the living, not on what the dead can still take an interest in.
Remembering someone, we speak of what *he* would have wished,
were he alive. There is no literal sense in which his continuing interests
can be served,[4] though we equivocate in speaking of his "interests." In
fact, we equivocate in another respect with regard to his will, shifting
between what the dead man has avowed in a formal way or in a final
moment (no matter how silly or pointless, within limits) and what,
were he rational, competent, and informed in the circumstances, he
would have chosen (no matter how remote or unlikely). The same
ellipsis informs Solon's maxim: "Count that man happy whose life is
done," by which we are invited to consider the terrible reversals that
may befall a man during his life, certainly not that the end of life is the
point of life. So it is a confusion between life and death or a privileged
doctrine about what goes on beyond apparent death that leads us to
think of death as a *personal state* of some sort inviting appraisal in the
same terms that obtain for life itself.

The required distinctions are clear enough but easily confused. A
man, living on, sees death as threatening an important and worth-

while venture or as threatening life itself, which he savors. Prospectively, *he* sees death as an evil. But, of course, anything may deflect
him from his project; so it is only relative to his personal, ongoing
objectives that death may be said to be an evil. If the project is important to others, then death is only accidentally an evil to them; and if it
was important only to the man who died, then the project is no longer
important because it is no longer important to him. Only if life is a good
in itself, not good merely because it is cherished, does the radical claim
have any plausibility. It is not that death is normal or inevitable that it is
not an evil. That poses no difficulty: men still count it, in prospect, an
evil. It is rather that it excludes the very condition of life on which the
personal appraisal of good and evil depends. It may be that the condition of dying is to be counted an evil, but the empirical evidence fails to
support even this thesis very strongly.[5] To count dying or aging or
suffering or ailing or the like as inherent evils is, effectively, to take the
human condition as evil; it is more like taking life as an evil than death.
But to count mere death as an evil is an utterly arbitrary or doctrinaire
view. It ignores just those contingent and personal concerns relative to
which it is normally so judged when it is so judged at all, or it imposes a
thesis about the inherent evil of the world. Actual death cannot be an evil
to the dead; and to the living, it signifies contingent deprivation within
the boundaries of life itself. Construing the alternatives thus, those
who hold mere death to be an evil are implicitly committed to regarding the world, on balance, as evil; and those who view death as an evil
relative to their ongoing objectives fail to assess death itself, except
accidentally.

What, then, is the significance of death?

First of all, it is significant that it is significant only for living human
beings. Only men, as we understand the matter at present, have the
full capacity to use language and, therefore, only men have the full
capacity to refer to themselves and to formulate thoughts of counter-
factual conditions or remote possibilities or the like. To think of one's
death is to think of a world in which, though one obviously still exists,
one no longer exists. Whatever may be true of one's speculations about
birth, which depend on the same distinction, only men must make
their commitments with the knowledge that they will die. Even if they
deny it, they must consider the matter. To fail to do so seems incompatible with the very concession of a sustained ability to refer to
oneself and the hazards of realizing that, whatever one undertakes,
one may not live long enough to complete a venture or to undertake a
new one. A minimal rationality, embodied in the capacity to use lan-

guage and to refer to oneself, must, faced with the hazards of life, reflect on the prospect of one's death.

We are quite naturally led to a second consideration. Birth focuses our extraordinary dependence on the antecedent activities of others and the arbitrary "selection" of our personal setting, our talents, and our opportunities. Death does not seem so arbitrary, unless it is the time or place of death or unless a special theory decides the issue: on the first view, we retreat to deprivation again; on the second, to privileged doctrine. Even Gilgamesh is more perceptive, for he comes to understand the"meaninglessness" of death. The significance of death, then, lies in its having no discoverable significance, no ulterior meaning in terms of the values the dead are deprived of, or in terms of a secret plan that, living and dying, we somehow serve. The meaning of death is just that it is the natural limit of life—natural, since we have no evidence of an animal stock that is immortal. The span of human life is somewhat less than a hundred years. Exceptionally, some Ecuadorian Indian or some peasant from Soviet Azerbaijan lives to the age of one hundred and thirty-five. But we are not tempted by the prospect of immortality, at least on empirical grounds; the best we can visualize is a significant extension of life itself, which is to say that our science is Faustian. But to concede that much is to concede that the question of mortality remains the same—its urgency sometimes postponed, its poignancy inevitably heightened.

Third, the significance of death lies in its affecting whatever we take to be significant in life itself. Being the limit of life, death colors every serious engagement. The point has been beautifully put by Don Juan, the Yaqui sorcerer:

> "Look at me," he said, "I have no doubts or remorse. Everything I do is my decision and my responsibility. The simplest thing I do, to take you for a walk in the desert, for instance, may very well mean my death. Death is stalking me. Therefore, I have no room for doubts or remorse. If I have to die as a result of taking you for a walk, then I must die.
>
> "You, on the other hand, feel that you are immortal, and the decisions of an immortal man can be canceled or regretted or doubted. In a world where death is the hunter, my friend, there is no time for regrets or doubts. There is only time for decisions."[6]

The imminence of death, then, disqualifies certain beliefs and attitudes for the rational man. Under no circumstances does he have unlimited time to do whatever he may suppose to be important to undertake.

The concept of immortality, however, is a complex one. Sometimes, it signifies unending life—not eternity, which, if intelligible at all, signifies a shift in one's frame of reference or a shift in "levels of being." Immortality would eliminate death but not, for that reason, the problem of the meaning of life; and in fact, in some mythologies, immortality does not even preclude death: the immortals are simply reborn unendingly, which provides the meaning of the cycle or else generates the same question. But immortality may also signify, as it obviously does in Don Juan's analysis, the opportunity to undo whatever one has at an earlier moment undertaken. Hence, immortality is often naively seen as magical power capable of completing all one's ventures indefinitely extended. Not that men actually believe themselves to be immortal; only that, failing to take cognizance of death, they act as if they were immortal.

So the significance of death lies in our appreciation, living, that we pass through the successive moments of our life but once (which, alternatively put, comes to an appreciation of the directionality of time) and that that sequence has a distinctly short, finite limit. In this sense, the significance of death is simply the finitude of life self-consciously infecting action and reflection. Needless to say, the fact of death cannot be merely acknowledged as a fact among others; it must be articulately linked to one's vision of the positive values of life. According to Nietzsche, the wisdom of Silenus teaches us that it is best not to be born at all and, failing that, to end one's life. We need a positive doctrine even to make suicide rational; and suicide, like its repudiation, acknowledges the inevitability of death. So there is a sense in which the bare fact of death has the same significance for all, even though no man can consider death an isolated fact unrelated to his personal convictions. We cannot consider impending death alone, since to do so is psychologically incompatible with the commitments of ongoing life; but the mere fact of death has a significance for all men alike and, minimally, the same significance.

Fourth, the significance of death lies in the reminder, conveyed by another's death, of one's own mortality. Here is the double edge of bereavement: a significant loss to the living, and a reminder that others will inevitably be confronted with one's own death. The fact has a personal force through every ceremony of grief, however austere or baroque it may be. Also, against Heidegger, there need be no equivocation on "death" in speaking of one's own and another's death: we attend to the death of other persons; and our own, in prospect, entails the dissolution of the body.[7] It is perhaps a natural extension to consider the mortality of aggregates and the metaphorical mortality of collective entities, like nations and civilizations. Sometimes, the connection is explicit, as in Spengler; sometimes, implicit, as in Ecclesiastes. It makes no difference. The essential point remains the same, the ubiquity of the import of death, the end of individuals and the reduction of the aggregates of which they are a part.

There is nothing that men may undertake that is not touched with the sense of their mortality. But its pressure is inescapably personal as well as social, simply because it collects the race, reflectively, in terms of an undeniably universal condition of the greatest importance. Birth collects us, too; but since it precedes the very sense of self-identity, it has an alien ring. Death is what every man faces in every encounter, regardless of whatever else may be at stake. Birth is more remotely connected with our lives, linked as it is with social history and the past. Death is directly implicated in every venture. Both murder and war, on the one hand, and the service and care of humanity and one's own intimates, on the other, are uniquely informed by the fact of mortality. Murder cuts down those whose existence interferes with the personal plans of other mortals; war pits mortal aggregates against one another in terms of the metaphorical immortality of their collective lives; and humanity to man, both near and far, is premised on sharing more or less equally and fairly, for the small interval we have, the very goods of life. It is possible that the murderer rages against his own finitude or that the samaritan and philanthropist comfort themselves. In any case, we recognize ourselves and one another as the mortal victims and beneficiaries of analogous acts, the neutral and original insight of every ideology and creed. "The slayer and the slain are one," so seen, simply projects an exhalted myth from a homely truth. The ease that infects our lives, confronted with the immanence of death, largely depends on the effectiveness with which we share the comforting doctrines our own society provides.

Finally, the significance of death lies in its not invalidating the significance of life. The race does not suicide simply because it becomes aware of its own mortality. On the contrary, it endlessly invents a conceptual rule for the acceptance of death. Extravagance is possible—perhaps, even necessary. But human life cannot ignore its own end, and even the most flat and apparently neutral acknowledgement is premised on the positive quality of life itself. In fact, the celebration of death can be nothing if not the celebration of life. We are forced to consider the merit of life. To construe it as a "gift" is to theorize about birth and about its inherent worth. But no sustained tradition has been capable of tolerating any and all uses of the putative gift. Directions are laid down for the proper use of life, inevitably for the end of life as well. The right way to die is simply a distinction within the general account of the right way to live. The point is that it cannot be ignored: since dying is a form of living, death provides no threatening complication. The trouble is that we are unable to *discover*, except subscribing to varied and incompatible higher Truths, what the proper use of life is. For that reason, death marks not only the significance of life, whatever we may allege it is, but also that life's significance lies in inventing and "discovering" again and again this or that significance.

There is a point to be pressed here. Otherwise, the fivefold significance of death would be a dubious contribution. Wisdom literature has plagued and comforted the world for ages. What we wish to know are the ineliminable implications of the fact that man knows he will die. Only in this way can we escape tendentious and partisan commitments, which we may well undertake for other reasons, and appreciate the force of the most powerful traditions addressed to the very fact of death. The point is simply this: every effort to specify the significance of death construes it in strictly formal terms, unless we presuppose, by some privileged access, that we already know its true significance. Death is significant to men alone. It has no significance except as the end of life. Its significance lies in affecting whatever is taken to be significant in life itself. Death is significant in that the death and mortality of others compel us to acknowledge our own, and our own compels us to acknowledge that of every other creature. Whatever its significance may be, it does not invalidate but is subsumed under the significance of life. We may say, then, that the significance of death is purely formal, has no doctrinal content at all. Or, we may say that death has no significance.

What is absolutely crucial to understand is that *no internally coherent policy or commitment whatsoever is rationally precluded by man's understanding that he must die.* Human beings can do anything at all consistently with the acknowledgement of mortality. Death forces us to shore up, personally and aggregatively, the convictions of life; that we persist and survive, as at least minimally rational creatures, confirms the pragmatic adequacy of our beliefs. And though the amplified doctrines to which we subscribe may forbid or permit this or that way of living or this or that way of dying, nothing whatsoever of such constraints may be derived from the ubiquity of death. Hence, the flowering of a thousand cultures. In this sense, death is not a morally significant fact: there are no rules that derive from it alone. In another sense, of course, it is the most momentous fact confronting every man.

The formality of the significance of death is matched by the formality of the significance of life. Taken in its most general form, capturing both

personal and political activity, the significance of life has traditionally
been expressed in versions of the doctrine of human or natural rights.
To be sure, such doctrines contain implications drawn from the hopes
and fears of partisan advocates. Still, as both the Declaration of
Independence and the Constitution of the United States make clear
(almost at the start of the modern practice of written constitutions),
basic human rights are merely formal and, in a sense, vacuous. Consider that the "right of life" simply stipulates a condition, life itself,
which every positive doctrine regarding personal and political conduct
presupposes in order merely to be a human option. Were there no men,
there would be no question of rights; since men pursue their objectives,
they must be alive to do so. Men must have a "right" to life if they have
any rights at all. But if one supposes that, in a just war, no one's right
to life is actually forfeited—or in justified capital punishment, or in the
tolerated misfortune of slavery or hopeless poverty or disease, or in unequal exploitation or the like—then the right to life is nothing but the
determinable condition of anyone who happens to be physically alive.
Otherwise, to speak of a "right" is simply to avoid arbitrariness, to
treat men similarly in whatever respects, yet to be designated, they are
said to be relevantly similar.[8] What every man within a given context is
said to be entitled to, as his right to life, is nothing but the partisan
embodiment of the minimal, the merely determinable, the so-called
"human" or "natural," right to life.

For example, if, in accord with the Universal Declaration of Human
Rights (adopted by the General Assembly of the United Nations in
1948), it is required that "No one shall be held in slavery or servitude;
slavery and the slave trade shall be prohibited in all their forms," the
constraint will be compatible only with certain theories about the *proper*
norms and objectives of human existence, theories open to dispute in a
way the merely determinable "right" of life could not be. The same is
true of the right of liberty, the right to property, and the right to pursue
one's own happiness. Again, the point is clear in Article 13 of the
Declaration: "Everyone has the right to leave any country, including
his own, and to return to his country." No country subscribing to the
Declaration would admit that to restrict the travel of its own citizens
and subjects violated *determinable* human rights (or even the narrower
rights of the Declaration) or that *determinate* legal rights were incompatible with those others. The only way to speak of violating human rights
is to speak of violating determinate legal or moral rights, which, on
some favored doctrine, entails the other.

The point is that the significance of life and death is entirely formal.
Neither from the mere fact that human beings are living creatures nor

from the fact that they must die does anything follow respecting normative values except what is entirely formal. Human rights are formal, but not constitutional or legal or civil rights or the rights posited by some well-established tradition, simply because the former collect only what is minimally entailed by the very fact that the vitality of men commits itself to the pursuit of *some* positive and sustained objective: doing so *is* to be alive. Anything less is tantamount to a denial of distinctly human life; anything more is tantamount to advancing a privileged and partisan doctrine. Emphasis on rights concerns only consistency of usage under *whatever* doctrinal restrictions are provided; it has nothing to say about the defensibility of any such restrictions, unless circularly, by appeal to the very doctrine by which given determinate rights are themselves established. And the fact of death is similarly formal because it points to no more than the fact that, whatever it may be, the significance of life is touched by the inescapable truth that men are mortal.

But we have looked at death exclusively from a first-person or personal vantage. In our own time, new complications arise because of the achievements of medical technology. For one thing, we are puzzled about fixing the limit of life that actually is death. And for another, we are puzzled about how to treat human beings in the state of dying, whose lives are maintained artificially and whose organs may be supposed to be of potential use to others.[9] The complications are enormous.

We must consider the tendency of medical and legal definitions of death to diverge under the pressure of new technologies, and the confusing distinctions between the "life" of organs suitable for transplant and the life of human beings—correspondingly, the so-called death of cells, the death of the lungs, the heart, and the brain, and the death of men. On the traditional medical view, according to Paul Ramsey, "death means the permanent disintegration and cessation of the spontaneous and integrated functions of intake, distribution, and utilization of oxygen . . . [which] may happen within the system beginning with the destruction of the brain's utilization of oxygen; or it may happen by respiratory blockage or by cardiac arrest. The destruction of one leads finally to the abolition of the others of these vital functions."[10] The trouble is that, although there are clear cases of death that satisfy this condition, regardless of the latest medical advances, technology can provide important borderline cases that call for revision of either the definition or the criteria of death or both.

There is one decisive issue that concerns us: the force of the traditional definition, which is fair enough, rests on the interpretation of the phrase "spontaneous and integrated functions." No matter how involved the medical or legal discussion of the propriety of using artificial means for maintaining life may be, the fact remains that the phrase "spontaneous and integrated functions" cannot, for borderline cases, but be normatively construed. A patient with a pacemaker cannot recover the "spontaneous" or "integrated" functioning of his heart *if* that means functioning without a pacemaker; and the patient in an iron lung cannot recover the "spontaneous" or "integrated" functioning of his lungs if that means functioning without an iron lung or functioning without a lung *for a relevant interval of time.* Ramsey, both somewhat favorably disposed to, and cautious about, the so-called Harvard Report,[11] says flatly that "I see no reason why an *entirely artificial* sustenance of breathing (and consequently of heartbeat) in an unburied corpse should be believed to be maintaining its 'life' even to the extent the Harvard committee allows by using the word in quotation marks."[12] But exactly when an "entirely artificial" sustenance is involved is rather difficult to decide; it is impossible to decide, in borderline cases, without reference to moral and related norms. If we imagine transistorized pacemakers, iron lungs, and even brain vivifiers all attached to a human being who would otherwise undoubtedly be dead, whose brain, lung, and heart functions could not otherwise be recovered or be "spontaneous" or "integrated," *but who can function with these devices in a way that favorably compares with the lives of others not so equipped,* we see that the determination of death depends on the practical and prudential interests of given communities of men. It is and cannot but be a question of our normative values, which, since such values inform medicine as well, preclude construing the question as a merely professional medical question.[13] Alternatively put, the apparent medical judgment is often nothing but a normative judgment of some more fundamental sort—call it prudential or moral —expressed in medical terms. This is clearly implied in the Harvard Report's distinctions bearing on clinical signs of death:

> (1) no receptivity or responsivity, complete lack of response to the most intensely painful external stimuli and complete lack of any manifestation of "inner need"; (2) no movement or breathing. Here we can see the meaning of "inner need": the total absence of spontaneous respiration in a patient on a mechanical respirator is established if, when the respirator is turned off for three minutes, there is "no effort" on the part of the patient to breathe spontaneously. Presumably the slightest effort to breathe (not success in doing so) would be taken as evidence of brain life, and *assisted* (as distinct from entirely artificial) respiration would be resumed; (3) no reflexes; and (4) flat electroencephalogram.[14]

We need not confuse the sense and criteria of death, for instance, as affecting the test of the three-minute interval or the repetition of the test at least once again after twenty-four hours. The thesis that machines *assist* rather than *artificially sustain* life, that there be some "effort" though perhaps no "success" of the *spontaneous* functioning of the vital organs, that the functioning be satisfactorily *integrated*, is, quite plainly, a purely verbal formula for marking what a medically informed community will allow its own medical professionals to treat as the distinction between life and death. The question is not one of the theoretical demarcation of the "moment of death."[15] It is rather one of the implicit normative instructions that a community gives to its practical specialists when informed of the latest technological possibilities.

Contrary to Ramsey's view, the definition of death is a moral matter affecting medicine, not merely a medical question that, consequentially, has moral implications. This is the decisive matter about which medical specialists and their most serious critics have been regularly misled. Theologians and moralists usually try to sensitize physicians to the moral implications of their own professional findings: what they fail to notice is that there can be no relevant findings unless and until the appropriate norms have been provided, and that those norms cannot be straightforwardly discovered by the medical profession itself. We are forever obliged to bear in mind that an unexpected turn in our technology may force us to reconsider any and all definitions of death; the best that informed professionals can accomplish in this regard is to recast distinctions in accord with the relevant norms that prevail in the society at large. But that, precisely, is to say that the question is not essentially a professional question. In the past, the concept of death was construed as morally neutral precisely because of our technological limitations; though to say this is not to deny that the taking of one's own or another's life and the care of the dying were always morally relevant issues. Now that our technology directly affects the specification of death itself and the reversibility, in various regards, of conditions previously thought to be sufficient for death's obtaining, we cannot any longer construe the concept as morally or normatively neutral. It is now impossible to deny that the question of sustaining life and postponing death by the latest technological means concerns a society's selective use of seriously limited facilities. To redefine death, within the context of our competence to sustain bodily functions, *is* simply to make an informed ethical decision. No more and no less. The point of emphasis, of course, is on the margin of our technological competence: a body that has been dead for three years, say, may be judged to be dead without involving any moral considerations; and the decision to end life, without broaching the question of redefinition, remains a moral question as before.

Finally, we may observe that the definition of death is a matter quite different from that of man's facing his own mortality. Men die and know that they do, regardless of when, precisely, death occurs or in what, precisely, death consists. So we may say, without contradiction, that the fact of mortality is significant in the purely formal sense that death is the inescapable limit of life, that mortality does not favor one set of values over another; while at the same time we maintain that the definition of death is, ultimately, a moral or prudential matter, not a matter of mere medical discovery or of the professional refinement of purely medical distinctions. The reason is simply that living men face the prospect of their own death. That is, living, they are also dying. But no one is ever called upon to judge that he himself is dead.

Notes

1. Cf. Paul Edwards' article, "My Death," in Paul Edwards, ed., *The Encyclopedia of Philosophy,* vol. 5 (New York: Macmillan, 1967), pp. 416-19.

2. The view here rejected has been recently suggested by Henry W. Johnstone, Jr., in an unpublished paper, "Sleep and Death," in which the impossibility of conceiving one's own birth or death is advanced. Compare Sigmund Freud, "Thoughts for the Times on War and Death" (1915), in *Collected Papers,* vol. 4, trans. J. Riviere (London: Hogarth Press, 1925). Cf. Ludwig Wittgenstein, *Tractatus,* trans, D.F. Pears and B.F. McGuinness (London: Routledge and Kegan Paul, 1961); *Lectures and Conversations on Aesthetics, Psychology and Religious Belief,* ed. C. Barrett (Oxford: Basil Blackwell, 1966); Warren Shibles, "Wittgenstein," in *Death* (Whitewater: The Language Press, 1974).

3. See, for instance, Paul Tillich, *The Courage To Be* (New Haven: Yale University Press, 1952).

4. Contrast Thomas Nagel, "Death," reprinted (somewhat enlarged) in James Rachels, ed., *Moral Problems* (New York: Harper and Row, 1971).

5. See Robert Kastenbaum and Ruth Aisenberg, *The Psychology of Death* (New York: Springer, 1972). Perhaps the most intimate account of dying appears in Elisabeth Kübler-Ross, *On Death and Dying* (New York: Macmillan, 1969). The thesis that death is an evil appears in Nagel, "Death"; also, in Paul Ramsey, "The Indignity of 'Death with Dignity,' "*The Hastings Center Studies* 2(1974): 47-62. Ramsey tends to blend the conceptual aspects of death, dying, and mortality with normatively satisfactory responses to these conditions. Thus, he rejects the consolation provided by the Epicurean finding that death is not a part of life, the finding by the "death with dignity" movement that dying is a part of living, and Wittgenstein's finding that living has no experienced limit. But the consolation offered rests on discoveries that are in themselves normatively neutral; also, Ramsey fails to demonstrate that it is, in some sense, *invalid* or how a valid mode of consolation could be provided. He urges us, merely as a partisan, to regard death as "evil," "the enemy," "the final indignity," so that some sense can be given to "overcoming" or "conquering" death; he also fears that his own conception is slowly being replaced. Cf. Leon R. Kass, "Averting One's Eyes, or Facing the Music?—on Dignity in Death," *The Hastings Center Studies* 2(1974): 67-80; and his "A Plea for Beneficent Euthanasia," *The Humanist* 34(1974): 4-5.

6. Carlos Castaneda, *Journey to Ixtlan* (New York: Simon and Schuster, 1972), p. 62. See also Edith Wyschogrod, "Sport, Death, and the Elemental," in Edith Wyschogrod, ed., *The Phenomenon of Death* (New York: Harper and Row, 1973).

7. See Edwards, "My Death."

8. Joseph Margolis, *Values and Conduct* (New York: Oxford University Press, 1971), Ch. 10.

9. Probably the most sustained recent discussion of these matters, also, clearly sorted, is to be found in Paul Ramsey, *The Patient as Person* (New Haven: Yale University Press, 1970), especially Chs. 2-3. See also Paul Ramsey, "On Updating Death," in Donald A. Cutler, ed., *Updating Life and Death* (Boston: Beacon Press, 1968). Ramsey cites the German theologian Helmut Thielicke, speaking of transplants, to the effect that we are concerned with "the vital conservation of single organs of an unburied corpse"; he also stresses, usefully, that "no longer to oppose death is not the same as first declaring a patient to be dead," p. 46. Cf. V. A. Nogovskii, *Resuscitation and Artificial Hypothermia*, trans. Basil Haigh (New York: Consultants Bureau, 1962), cited by Kastenbaum and Aisenberg, *The Psychology of Death*.

10. Ramsey, *The Patient as Person*, p. 64.

11. "A Definition of Irreversible Coma," *Journal of the American Medical Association* 205(1968): 85-88.

12. Ramsey, *The Patient as Person*, p. 94. A comparable problem arises, of course, in determining when abortion may be practiced (if in principle allowed) where considerations of the fetus' "humanity" are involved—for instance, at quickening or viability; see Sissela Bok, "Ethical Problems of Abortion," *The Hastings Center Studies* 2(1974): 33-52.

13. See Joseph Margolis, *Psychotherapy and Morality* (New York: Random House, 1966); "Illness and Medical Values," *The Philosophy Forum* 8(1969): 55-76; and *Values and Conduct*.

14. Ramsey, *The Patient as Person*, p. 92. See also Ivan Illich, "The Political Uses of Natural Death," *The Hastings Center Studies*, 2(1974): 3-20, for a survey of the changing image of medicine's role regarding death. It should be emphasized that the coma may, on the criteria given, be detected independently of its "irreversibility": irreversibility apparently is operationally determined by the failure of the tests in "repeated examinations over a period of 24 hours or longer" ("A Definition of Irreversible Coma"). See also Henry K. Beecher, "Definitions of 'Life' and 'Death' for Medical Science and Practice," *Annals of the New York Academy of Sciences* 169(1970): 471-74.

15. Ramsey, *The Patient as Person*, pp. 63-64.

2

Suicide

Suicide is thought to provide a telling test for a moral theory because, unlike murder, it is problematic whether and how it can be plausibly condemned. As far as linguistic usage goes, there is no clear sense in which characterizing an act as an act of suicide entails its being blameworthy, evil, sinful, or reprehensible. Not that suicide is not reprehensible: it may or it may not be. But that cannot be decided merely by labeling it as such. It is true the expression "self-murder" had currency in an earlier age; but that signifies either that suicide was viewed as murder within a particular tradition, or that the particular manner in which one took his life, though admittedly suicide, was also reprehensible (for instance, in order to avoid obligations as a soldier in battle).[1]

An initial difficulty in deciding the issue concerns the sorting of specimen instances. A man may knowingly and willingly go to his death, be rationally capable of avoiding death, deliberately not act to save his life, and yet not count as a suicide. In this sense, we usually exclude the man who sacrifices his life to save another's, the religious martyr who will not violate his faith, the patriot who intentionally lays down his life for a cause. Not that men in such circumstances may not be suiciding; only that they cannot be said to be suiciding solely for those reasons. Some seem to have thought otherwise. "Suicide," says Emile Durkheim, "is applied to all cases of death resulting directly or indirectly from a positive or negative act of the victim himself, which he knows will produce this result."[2] So there may be an element of arbitrariness in including or excluding specimens. We can expect a theory of suicide to be applicable only relative to the cases admitted, but we may quarrel about the inclusion or exclusion of given cases. General Custer, for instance, is sometimes thought, on psychoanalytic grounds, to have had a pronounced death wish; consequently, on a strenuous theory involving unconscious acts, he is supposed to have suicided at Little Bighorn. Clearly, what we want to accommodate are the relatively undisputed and central cases.

Sometimes, quite reasonably, it is supposed that there is a fundamental difference between suicide religiously and non-religiously construed. R.F. Holland, for instance, believes there is such a difference.[3] On his view, the suicide is religiously condemned because he is an ingrate respecting a gift his Creator has given him. Holland seems not to have taken seriously enough the fact that the Stoics, unlike the Christians, took their lives with ritual equanimity. The Stoics were hardly behaving as ingrates—on the contrary, they may have been celebrating their own divinity as fulgurations of the divine fire of Reason. In a related though distinct spirit, the self-immolation of Vietnamese priests and the hara-kiri of the Japanese novelist Yukio Mishima conformed to the highest religious sensibilities of their tradition. Holland also speaks of a so-called humanist, that is, non-religious, attitude toward suicide: for him, it is embodied in the case of a man with terminal cancer, all his faculties intact, whose sense of the worth of life gave him a reason for suiciding when he "saw . . . no sense in prolonging his life beyond a certain point." The case is a fair and important one, of course; but in what sense, on the hypothesis, has an *ethical* justification been provided? We understand why the man acted as he did, but how did his sense of the worth of his life or of life itself justify his suiciding? And why should Holland insist that the "humanist" suicide had to view the world as he did? Could he not have decided that life was utterly meaningless? Could he not have found life to be utterly meaningless for him? If one could justify suicide in the terminal cancer case, how much more convincingly could a man justify suicide if he sincerely believed life to have no point at all? In fact, as a rational agent, believing life to be meaningless, would he not, as Nietzsche supposed, be obliged to suicide?

The point of pressing these obvious considerations is to bring home the culturally variable character of suicide. There is no bare religious or non-religious view of suicide—there are many competing views, some religious, some not, some not even significantly so characterized. Every relevant instance collects a highly institutionalized tradition. There are paradigms of admissible Buddhist, Shinto, Stoic, Epicurean suicides; and, in terms that, for doctrinal reasons, cannot be construed as suicide but that involve very many of the same elements, there are, in the Christian and Muslim traditions, admissible ways of ending or yielding one's life that could be avoided on the option and action of the person affected. There is perhaps not that much difference between the action of the kamikaze pilot and the Christian crusader or the Muslim warrior seeking death in battle against the infidel. But in the Christian and Muslim traditions, to construe the activity involved as suicide would be to condemn the agent. So, for example, the martyr who yields his life to his tormentors is said not to be a suicide; though if, under the same pressure, he ended his life by his sword, he would have been a suicide. Socrates took his life by drinking the cup of hemlock and did not simply yield his life to others, and is said, in accord with another tradition, not to have suicided; yet, the Athenians were obviously hoping that Socrates would have taken the option open to him to leave the city forever. In Eskimo society, the elderly will take a small supply of food and leave their community never to return, anticipating that they will die in a matter of days. They will not take their own lives by a direct physical act but they will put themselves in the position of imminent and inevitable death; yet, they are usually not said to have committed suicide. Here, it seems undeniable that we either respect the favorable judgment or approval of the home culture and therefore refuse to label the act suicide in order not to raise the prospect (or the certainty) of condemning it in accord with our own conceptual preferences; or, viewing it favorably in terms of our own values, we refuse to label it such in order to avoid the same prospect. Socrates, we say, upheld the judgment of the Athenian court; and, having done so, he found the option of leaving the city meaningless, morally unacceptable, or repugnant. The Eskimo, we say, respected the implications of the marginal existence of his community and acted to permit others a more realistic distribution of food when he was no longer able to contribute useful labor; in doing so, he rejects as morally unacceptable whatever it would take to force others to provide for his own life under the general condition of mortality.

There is no reason to dispute these assessments. In fact, what is important is the force of their admission. There is no simple formula for designating, except trivially, an act of taking, or yielding, or making likely the end of, one's life that will count, universally, as suicide. No, some selection of acts of this minimal sort will, in accord with an interpreting tradition, construe what was done as or as not suicide; and, so judging, the tradition will provide as well for the approval or condemnation of what was done. In short, suicide, like murder itself, is an act that can be specified only in a systematic way within a given tradition; and that specification itself depends on classifying the intention of the agent. We can say, therefore, that there is no minimal act of commission or omission that counts as suicide, except relative to some tradition; and, within particular traditions, the justifiability of particular suicides may yet be debatable.

There is, however, one way of characterizing suicide that, though it goes counter to some familiar judgments, manages to isolate as neutrally as possible the issue most in dispute: whether the deliberate taking of one's life in order simply to end it, not instrumentally for any ulterior purpose, can ever be rational or rationally justified. Durkheim's alternative characterization resolves the issue trivially, since, as in the case of a spy's taking his life to avoid capture or as in the case of sacrificing one's life for another, there could not but be, on Durkheim's criterion, ready cases of rational suicide. The trouble is that Durkheim's criterion does not enable us to focus the point of the serious charge that suicide is never rational or rationally justified. We shall, therefore, construe suicide as narrowly as possible in order to allow the issue a fair inning: we can thereafter, of course, always temper our classification in the direction of Durkheim's view—with the consequence of being increasingly unable to generalize meaningfully about the phenomenon itself. Thus construed, we shall take it that to characterize an act as an act of suicide is to describe it in a way that takes precedence over every alternative characterization. If Socrates is said not to have suicided, it is because what he did is described overridingly as adhering to the rules of Athenian justice: that characterization precludes his having suicided. We cannot hold consistently that Socrates suicided but was justified in doing so because, in so doing, he upheld Athenian justice overridingly. Obviously, in taking his life, he upheld Athenian justice. But to judge that he suicided is to render a verdict, all things considered, that disallows ascribing a merely *instrumental* purpose or intention to the act in question; to judge that, acting as he did, he supported Athenian justice is to assign Socrates an overriding and ulterior objective inconsistent with intending suicide. The suicide's overriding concern is to end his own life, not for the sake of any independent objective that, in principle, he might pursue in another way: he is persuaded there is no other commitment that, under the circumstances, would command his rational assent, and he knows that a successful act precludes any further commitment on his own part.

There is, here, a small but crucial puzzle to be resolved. If the Muslim warrior actively seeks to lose his life against the infidel, and, in this sense, suicides for the sake of instant salvation, we seem to have violated the constraint just imposed. But this confuses the doctrine in terms of which particular instances of suicide are identified and interpretively characterized and the ulterior and independent objectives that taking or yielding one's life may instrumentally serve. For instance, the spy who takes his own life to keep strategic secrets from the enemy has not suicided though he has taken his life: he has, as we say, sacrificed his life for the sake of national security or to fulfill his supposed duty, which could not entail taking his own life as such. Our characterization ordinarily precludes suicide. If, however, we say that the Muslim suicided and, in so doing, acted to insure his salvation, then we must, for the sake of consistency, construe his act as a *sui generis* ritual suicide, as an act that is essentially a way of insuring salvation. This shows the variety of formulas available for characterizing acts of taking or yielding one's life.

The Buddhist monk who sets fire to himself in order to protest the war that he might have resisted in another way will not be said to have committed suicide if the *overriding* characterization of what he did fixes on the ulterior objective of influencing his countrymen. But he *may* be said to have suicided if resisting the war and influencing his countrymen are judged not to bear on what, all things considered, proves to be the overriding characterization of what he did; *and*, if he is said to have suicided even though he took his life in order to protest the war, then there is no coherent way to view his act but as an act of protest-suicide, a ritualized act of suiciding whose essential import, given the relevant doctrine, is that of protest. Thus, to say that the Buddhist monk suicided for the sake of protesting the war is to ascribe a certain intrinsic quality to the act itself; and to say that he suicided, rather than took or sacrificed his life, in order to gain the independent objective of influencing his countrymen is to contradict oneself. In pursuing an ulterior objective by way of taking one's own life, one's efforts are instrumentally related to that independent objective. Suicide supersedes every instrumental use of one's own life; only its intrinsic import remains to be considered. Exotic cases are really no different from the case of the man with terminal cancer. Against Kant and

Schopenhauer, the cancer patient has not taken his life merely to reduce his pain; he has taken it in order to end it. If the monk's act is protest-suicide, the other's is termination-of-meaningless-suffering-suicide. Alternatively put, when we say that a man has committed suicide in order to avoid pain, or a spy, to avoid capture by the enemy, we mean to say that he killed himself or deliberately allowed his life to be taken and that his act served an ulterior purpose. But to speak in this way is to speak elliptically, in effect, avoiding a full verdict or rendering one of another kind. For, if the spy sacrificed his life, then either he did not suicide, suicide being precluded, or else the ascription merely signifies responsibility for his own death, inviting but not constituting a verdict; and if a man takes his life to avoid pain, then either he is irrational, failing to see that suicide cannot secure that further objective, namely, his being in a painless state after the act, or else life has become meaningless to him or not worth living or the like because of the pain. So an irrational suicide may well intend to act instrumentally, failing to construe his behavior thus; but to speak of a rational suicide entails conceptual constraints on a range of arguable cases. Also, one cannot suicide merely for another's benefit: rationally, one must have judged that he ought to end his life, thinking, in addition, that his death would benefit another.

The critical distinctions are these: if an agent is presumed rational, then if he takes his own life or allows it to be taken for some further purpose that he serves instrumentally, then we normally refuse to say he has suicided; and if he is presumed irrational, then taking his own life in some putatively instrumental way is normally taken as suicide. This is the reason that, in the clinical professions, suicide tends to be linked to illness, weakness of character, insanity, or the like: any scanning of the psychiatric literature, for instance, confirms this.[4] But such a view utterly ignores the kind of cases, already sampled, in which people simply wish to put an end to their lives because life has ceased to have a sufficiently favorable significance or because taking one's life, under the circumstances, does have a sufficiently favorable significance.

These distinctions have considerable theoretical importance, for they show how easily the characterization of an act, in which some independent and ulterior consequence may be assigned, may be replaced by another that elides the act and its putative consequence.[5] Obviously, the appraisal of a man's action, depending as it does on variable characterizations of what he has done, is open to a variety of values. Treat the monk's act as an act of sacrifice, and questions of patriotism and altruism obtain; treat it as an act of suicide and questions of piety and sanity obtain. There appears to be no neutral ground on which, not subscribing to this or that disputed theory, the act in question may be characterized *as* sacrifice or suicide. Suicide is an interpretive category imposed on acts, characterizable in relatively neutral ways, in accord with a relevant doctrine or ideology.

A rational suicide, then, may fairly be said to be a person who aims overridingly at ending his own life and who, in a relevant sense, performs the act. The manner in which he suicides may be said to be by commission or omission, actively or passively, directly or indirectly, consciously or unconsciously, justifiably or reprehensibly—in accord with the classificatory distinctions of particular traditions. Spinoza holds the drive to survive essential to human nature; reason, serving this *conatus* in man, cannot prefer suicide. Hence, he judges suicide to be inherently irrational. By a small adjustment, Freud, a true Spinozist, was inclined to view intended suicide as a form of illness. Orthodox Freudians find it almost impossible not to suppose, even in the absence of evidence, that every would-be suicide has had a psychotic break that triggered his act. In any event, the concept of a rational suicide is thought by them to be self-contradictory. On that view, the possibility of an ethical appraisal of suicide is either obviated or very seriously restricted; for if a given case is a genuine case of suicide, the agent must have been irrational and only his responsibility for being irrational could remain a relevant issue. Hence, the attractiveness of viewing suicide as an illness: it justifies full public and professional concern (and control) where the usual notions of responsibility are inapt.

There is, however, an uneasy feeling that this way of proceeding is rather academic, since the successful suicide cannot possibly be an agent whose present or past behavior relevantly bears on his behavior in the future. In every other case but suicide, the loss of life is, by definition, not the overriding objective of one's act. Consequently, the ethical appraisal of an action that happens to entail one's ending his life cannot relevantly bear on whether suicide may be ethically condemned. It is in this sense that suicide is thought to test the competence of any moral theory; and it is for this reason that Durkheim, in effect, restricts his own definition in terms of considerations of *anomie*, that is, in ideological terms. Spinoza's view is at least arguable; but it is difficult to see how, on independent grounds, it can be shown that every suicide is inherently irrational. It may in fact be held that, on empirical evidence, men actually lose their *conatus*, their desire to live, actually find life meaningless without losing their reason. If this be admitted, then Spinoza is simply wrong, and rational suicide is possible; correspondingly, Freud is wrong and rational, sane, and normal suicide is possible.

Behind our alternative accounts—conventional, traditional, sometimes incompatible, in accord with which we affirm or deny that this or that was an act of suicide and, as such, is or is not to be approved or condemned—a deeper doctrine lurks, namely, that man's essential nature is such that suicide inherently violates or is inherently in accord with the functions of human nature. Even the Freudian or Spinozist need not be put off by the evidence that men sometimes profoundly believe that life is meaningless though they have not lost their reason; one has only to hold that this itself violates man's "essential" function. Of course, the Stoic will insist that suicide accords with that essential function. Hence, the quarrel about condemning suicide will merely be raised to a seemingly superior debate about man's essential nature. Here, it may be flatly said that there is no convincing way in which to determine or discover what the truly essential function of human nature is or what the natural norms are in accord with which human life ought to be lived. Every pretended formulation will simply qualify or disqualify competing views; and, by an absurd regress, we should have to quarrel about the "proper" way of discerning the "essential" function of man, with respect to which we could "properly" judge the justifiability of suicide. There is no upper limit to this spiralling inquiry, except imagination itself.

On the other hand, the effort to fix the normative import of man's very nature depends on a confusion about alternative classificatory procedures. For, although it is true that man *qua* physician, *qua* pilot, *qua* general, *qua* cobbler, *qua* shepherd has, drawing together all of Plato's disarming examples, an essential function with respect to which one may judge the functioning of any incumbent of a given role or office, there is no comparable sense in which man *qua* man may be so judged. Admittedly, the concept of a physician entails the concept of ministering to the health of patients; hence it entails functional norms with respect to which relevant appraisals may be made. But it is not logically necessary that all classificatory terms entail such norms, and a great many, including *man, baboon, lion,* and *dog,* appear to be regularly used in terms only of resemblances to standard instances not themselves gauged in terms of excellence or perfection of any sort.[6] Functions and obligations are assigned men in accord with their offices, roles, special relationships; additional obligations are assigned them in accord with privileged doctrines about the proper use of life. In this sense, condemning or approving suicide is a matter internal to quite particular traditions.

Now, if man had an essential function, it would be a straightforward matter to judge suicide ethically; we should have to consider only whether suicide was in accord with or contrary to the natural norms of human existence. But if man has no normatively significant nature as such, then of course it can only be in terms of influential doctrine that men are said to have a moral right or a moral duty respecting suicide.

There is some reason, however, to think that suicide is not a moral question. Every ethical concern, leaving suicide aside, presupposes some ongoing life or community of lives. The man who cheats is held responsible for what he has done, and reparations must be considered. The man who murders is held responsible for his act, and the restoration of public order is required. But suicide is unique, in the sense that what is intended is to affect one's own life only in an absolutely final way that eliminates the agent altogether. The ethical worth of sacrificing one's life or of taking another's is properly judged in accord with the consequences or import of that act for an ongoing community. What the judgment will be will vary from one tradition to another, but the relevance of an ethical appraisal will hardly be denied. In the case of suicide, it is not clear what or how ethical considerations *impinge.* If the suicide fails to pay his debts, for instance, or if the loss to those who remain concerns us, suicide will be only accidentally relevant; and if, on the hypothesis, only the agent's life calls for an ethical appraisal, then that is just what has been eliminated once and for all: appraisal of his life prior to suicide is irrelevant and appraisal of his life after suicide is impossible. The question is whether it is ethically right or wrong merely to suicide.

Also, to appreciate the narrowness of the question is to appreciate that men can suicide only as men: one cannot suicide as a functionary or as filling a certain role or office. For one thing, no one is exhausted by his roles or relationships; and what one does as a man takes precedence over what he does in any special capacity. For another, anyone who takes or yields his life because of what is right or required of him in a special capacity is said (*if* rational) not to have suicided but to have sacrificed his life or to have done his duty. The spy who takes his life to keep state secrets from the enemy sacrifices his life instrumentally; he devotes himself to his patriotic objective. The suicide acts as a whole man, not as a functionary; that is, he acts overridingly, all things considered, to end his life. It is absurd to suppose that a man would take or yield his life only instrumentally, viewing what he does only in terms of fulfilling some functionary duty. The same is true of taking another's life: the rational soldier, for instance, taking another's life *qua* soldier, knows that he takes the life of a man and not merely an enemy and knows that *he* as a man and not merely as a soldier takes another's life. So the spy and the soldier and the suicide, rationally, must construe what they do as the act of a man justified by considerations that take precedence over any and all merely functionary duties.

Viewed this way, the thesis that man has a right or a duty regarding suicide, whether suicide is permitted or required or whether one must or may forbear, is essentially the same issue. The man who has a right to suicide has a right that cannot be justified in terms of benefits to the community at large; and the man who has a duty to avoid suicide has a duty that cannot be justified in terms of obligations to others. The curious thing is that if it is held that men have an ethical right or duty respecting suicide, they have a right that, though the corresponding duties may be social, is a right that may be meaningfully exercised in total isolation from the rest of society and without any regard for the interests of others; or, in having a duty, they have a duty that they owe solely to themselves. If society confers a right or a duty respecting suicide, then, trivially, suicide is an ethical concern. But conferring such a right or a duty seems to exceed the competence of any aggregate of men, since it cannot be construed in terms of its import or consequences for the conferring society itself. There seems to be no rational basis on which a society could justify originating such a right or a duty. It could be claimed that it was entailed by the concept of human nature itself, but we have already seen the weakness of that line of reasoning; it could be claimed that it was promulgated by some divinity, but that line of reasoning precludes debate.

We may, then, formulate a conception of what a morally relevant issue is, congruent with the distinctions noted: it would exclude suicide as a moral issue but account for our moral concern with cases of suicide. Consider that, preponderantly, men act to preserve their lives, to reduce their suffering and pain, to gratify their desires selectively, to minimize unexpected change and risk respecting their objectives, to regularize relations with other human beings, to increase their power to achieve their objectives. We may call all such goals prudential and take it that pursuing prudential goals is statistically characteristic of human behavior. On such grounds, then, we posit a *prima facie* norm of *rationality*, namely, that acting in accord with prudential interests is, *prima facie*, acting rationally. This means that to explain why one has acted as he has by reference to the putatively prudential interests of the race is, to that extent, to provide sufficient reasons for so acting; to act rationally but contrary to such interests calls for an explanation in terms of other considerations. Minimally, moral questions concern the behavior of men acting in ways that impinge on the prudential interests of others. It is possible, of course, to act contrary to prudential interests and to be ethically justified in so doing; thwarting a thief, for instance, or sacrificing one's life for a good cause. But if that is so, then prudence and morality are not coextensive and an agent may act rationally though not prudently or not in accord with given prudential interests. Hence, suicide may be rational without being prudent and without being eligible for ethical approval or condemnation. Suicide does not concern the prudential interests of others, so it is not a moral matter; and, though it goes contrary to one's presumed prudential interests, it may do so rationally, as when life has lost its meaning and one knows himself to have discarded prudential interests. So seen, suicide may be construed as a moral issue only if men can be shown to have duties to themselves or functions essential to their nature as human beings.

Still, there are at least three reasons why we cannot ignore cases of suicide. For one, if morality concerns affecting the prudential interests of others, it is entirely possible that a bona fide act of suicide impinges, for other reasons, on the prudential interests of others. For a second, since moral issues presuppose prudential interests, we suppose any ethically responsible agent to be committed, *prima facie,* to respect his own prudential interests. Thus, a suicide may leave his family destitute and a man may lose his life through negligence or irrational behavior. In both instances, society acts custodially; in the first, with regard to those affected; in the second, to preserve agents from unwittingly or irrationally damaging themselves. Obviously, neither consideration bears directly on the ethical status of suicide, and on the thesis just proposed respecting what a moral question is, rational suicide remains outside the pale of moral approval or condemnation. It is conceptually impossible, admitting its coherence, to view rational suicide as self-damaging. Suicide does not entail the rejection of morality or reason, only of those prudential concerns that the very relevance of moral review presupposes. Nor is it a higher concern that takes precedence over the moral; it is perhaps a lower or more elemental, obviating the very point of the moral concern. Still, as in the case of the Buddhist monk, what is below and above morality may well converge.

There is, also, a third reason for an ethical interest in suicide, namely, that irrational suicide is often thought to be open to moral censure, not because of irrationality itself, which normally precludes responsibility, but because of a weakness of character that leads to an irrational act of suicide without producing an irrational nature. The man who takes his life out of extreme fear, say, as a soldier under fire, is normally censured for so behaving: that his act happens to be an act of suicide confirms his irrationality, since his only objective could have been to escape the cause of his fear and his not surviving nullifies his strategy; that he is to be censured as a moral coward confirms that his suicide is only accidentally relevant. It is only rational suicide, therefore, that falls outside the pale of moral approval and condemnation; but only a moral review shows it to be so.

One final consideration. Men are sometimes said to suicide as victims of a disturbed state of mind, in a fit of depression, or as the result of an unbearably prolonged depression. Here, we need to know whether the victim can be said to have had any reasons at all for suiciding or whether he was merely overwhelmed and acted entirely involuntarily.[7] This is not to deny the compatibility of reasons and causes, or freedom and causality, or rationalization and causal explanation.[8] But if the suicide is merely a victim of his own psychological state, then the question of defense and justification is precluded: we feel pity for his having "taken" his life thus, which is morally relevant; but, in a somewhat Aristotelian sense, his suicide is neither rational nor irrational, since his agency was so defective. If, on the other hand, he is somewhat the victim of his own state of mind, he may yet be said to have reasons for acting as he did; if so, then, to that extent we may consider his behavior as before, in accord with rational or irrational motivation. There seem to be no other kinds of cases to collect.

To put the argument concisely: we have provided a sense in which a man may be a rational suicide, the sense in which a man has as his overriding concern the ending of his life. This permits us to preclude all cases in which a man ends his own life merely instrumentally, unless irrationally. Rational suicide invites an appraisal of the import or quality of the act, not of its ulterior objectives. In this sense, the terminal cancer patient behaves in a way comparable to that of the Muslim warrior, though their beliefs are different. The patient's interests in surviving are drained; life has lost its meaning or savor; there are no further prudential interests he means to pursue. Marginally, perhaps, reducing pain, for instance, by prolonged anesthesia, is prudentially preferable to enduring pain; but in itself this cannot justify construing suicide to end pain as a decision of a prudential sort. The defense or censure of suicide is undertaken, of course, in doctrinal terms—religiously (by Stoics and Christians), ethically (as in humanist and Kantian accounts), aesthetically (as in Nietzsche and, perhaps, Schopenhauer). But the hard case is the case of the suicide not committed to some *justificatory* doctrine. He takes his life only to end it, not, necessarily, to avoid evil or to secure some good. In a sense, we can only explain why he has suicided: life doesn't attract him any longer or sufficiently to go on living. Counsels of caution or patience are impertinent, for he does no more than fix the limit of his own mortality. We may condemn or applaud him on doctrinal grounds. In his own terms, however, we note only that he has acted rationally: believing overridingly that there is no point to going on, he acts consistently. In this sense, rationality is deeper than prudence or morality, and none is equivalent to any other. Finally, the very category of suicide interprets, in terms of some selective doctrine, the intentions and conduct of agents said to have taken or to have attempted to take their own lives and to provide for the appraisal of those actions: there is no neutral concept of suicide, and what is allowed or disallowed as a fair specimen reflects at least conditions that alternatively favored creeds would have to meet in order to be minimally coherent, if it does not already exhibit their actual preferences.

Notes

1. See David Daube, "The Linguistics of Suicide," *Philosophy and Public Affairs* 1(1972): 387-437. Karl Menninger takes suicide to be "obviously a *murder* . . . committed *by* the self as murderer"; see his comments in Edwin S. Shneidman, Norman L. Farberow, and Robert E. Litman, eds., *The Psychology of Suicide* (New York: Science House, 1970), p. 38. *The Psychology of Suicide* is probably one of the most sustained studies of suicide available. It is interesting, therefore, that Shneidman, the principal author, finds "the word *suicide* currently has too many loose and contradictory meanings to be scientifically or clinically useful" (Ch. 1) and, in spite of (or perhaps because of) their long association with the Los Angeles Suicide Prevention Center, the authors attempt no sustained discussion of the defensibility or acceptability of suicide.

2. *Suicide,* trans. John A. Spaulding and George Simpson (New York: Free Press, 1951), p. 44.

3. See "Suicide," in *Talk of God,* Royal Institute of Philosophy Lectures, Vol. 2, 1967-68 (London: Macmillan, 1969).

4. Psychoanalytic resistance to the conception may be gauged in Joost A. M. Meerloo, *Suicide and Mass Suicide* (New York: E. P. Dutton, 1968), where considerable emphasis is placed on "the suicidal man within us," our inherent self-destructive urge. See Erwin Stengel, *Suicide and Attempted Suicide* (Hammondsworth: Penguin, 1964); Stengel offers the interesting thesis, again from a psychiatric and psychoanalytically oriented view, that "most people who commit suicidal acts do not either want to die or to live; they want to do both at the same time . . . " (p. 87)—that is, they are irrational. There is no doubt that suicide is often irrational, but the psychoanalytic accounts seem not to make any provision for rational suicide; hence, they tend to assimilate suicide to illness if not to insanity.

5. For further discussion, see Joseph Margolis, *Values and Conduct* (New York: Oxford University Press, 1971), Ch. 7.

6. See Margolis, *Values and Conduct,* Ch. 5.

7. See Sylvia Plath, *The Bell Jar* (New York: Harper and Row, 1971); and A. Alvarez, *The*

Savage God (London: Wiederfeld and Nicolson, 1971), especially "Prologue: Sylvia Plath."

8. See Joseph Margolis, "Puzzles about Explanation by Reasons and Explanation by Causes," *Journal of Philosophy* 67(1970): 187-95.

3

Abortion

The defense of abortion strains our moral sensibilities primarily because of the complexity of the ways in which our view of it is affected
by other relatively independent social themes. For instance, if the
world's population threatened to multiply dangerously within a generation, then routinized abortion might well be required in the interest
of racial survival; and that consideration might well be thought to take
precedence over the saving of any random fetus in any rationally
defensible policy. Also, if women could practice abortion easily and
effectively by themselves, by the use of a preparation available in
the supermarket, then the very privacy and ease of commission,
the difficulty of effective legal constraints, and widespread practice
typically without shame or a sense of guilt would probably conspire to
make the issue a matter of a woman's right over her own body or
a matter of conscience to be decided between herself and her family
or loved ones. Or, if fetuses were produced by artificial insemination
or even entirely outside the body of a woman, then the planning

entailed would probably persuade us both of the ease with which alternative fetuses could be provided and of the general irrelevance of the usual claims of the rights of the fetus in assessing whether the developing embryo is or is not acceptable on any given scale. Of course, abortion under such circumstances would not be open to discussion in terms of women's rights as currently construed, that is, in terms of the use of a woman's body. Again, if abortion is seen as a problem because, on some religious view, the unborn fetus cannot be baptized and yet, at a critical point in its development, at conception, quickening, birth, or when viable, it is said to have an immortal soul and therefore to require baptism, then there is an end to the debate in the double sense that the faithful have no recourse without a change in theology and those outside the faith can find no common ground for dispute.

These considerations show that the currently heated debate about abortion is peculiarly affected by comparatively temporary and highly changeable features of population density, technology, religious influence or the like. This is not to say that it is any the less serious for those features, but rather that it must be faced as an issue for a population neither too large nor too small to affect the form of the question decisively, whose relevant technology and socially endorsed practices have significantly changed in recent years but not too radically from what obtained in an earlier age, and whose ethical and religious convictions remain relevantly divided.

Having said this, we may conveniently add that the question of abortion is hardly interesting, conceptually, unless we admit that the fetus is a living human being, as yet unborn—redundantly, in this misleading sense, an *innocent* creature, a creature that has a "right to life" because to take its life calls for defending reasons, *not* in the sense that defending reasons are altogether impossible to provide. This is not to say that there is no morally relevant difference between an unborn fetus and a human infant or a human adult; nor that a fetus is human in every fair sense of the term; nor that a fetus is a person, that is, a sentient creature capable of using language.[1] It is only to say that, in taking the life of an unborn fetus, one must consider the possibility of defense in terms, minimally, of the fetus' belonging to the human species, that taking the life of another human being calls for ethical defense.[2]

Consequently, though it is obvious that there is a good deal of debate about *when*, in the developmental cycle of the fetus, it is appropriate to speak of its being an unborn human being, the issue is not really interesting except insofar as *deciding* where to draw the line signifies the point at which the important conceptual issues obtain. Under the circumstances, so deciding is itself an ethical concern. If, for example, on doctrinal grounds it is conceded that the fertilized ovum during the first week following conception is not yet a human being, then abortion cannot be construed in terms of the conflicting rights of a woman and the human fetus she bears. It would have to be subsumed, in whatever interesting way may obtain, under categories concerned exclusively with the well-being of the woman or family or race affected, without reference at all to the putative interests of the fetus. It is well known that the most incredible disputes have developed in religious circles, chiefly though not exclusively Roman Catholic, in fact now even among scientists in the biological disciplines, about when, precisely, to say the fetus is a human being.[3] But, of course, there is no purely scientific basis on which to determine when and when not the fetus is human, and religiously dictated decisions are not open to debate in the usual sense. The fertilized egg, after all, is a fertilized egg produced by two human beings or suitable surrogates, if we imagine our technology sufficiently advanced. Any self-consistent demarcation line will necessarily be consistent with whatever scientific data we may obtain, as long as we do not beg the question. There is no point to the biologist's pronouncing that the fertilized egg at this or that precise stage of development is an unborn human being; his definition is intended to have normative import, in the sense that the question of the defense of abortion thereupon obtains. Nothing that he discerns could not be admitted by another biologist who chose to draw the line at a different point. Certainly, the defense of abortion in particular cases will be affected by the admission that we are dealing with an unborn human being, but that is simply to say that the relevant ethical reflections will be brought to bear on these or those cases but not, perhaps, on those. Let us agree, then, that the fetus is an unborn human being, in order to see what may be said about the ethically interesting features of the practice of abortion.

One thing is apparent: we cannot, as we now understand the phenomenon, satisfactorily invoke the so-called Principle of Double Effect,[4] the distinction, relative to justifying deliberate acts, between intended and merely foreseen consequences. It cannot be maintained convincingly that abortion is designed solely to promote the well-being or life of the mother, where, in so doing, the life of the fetus will be ended. No, the causal connections are much too explicit and clear: one intends *to* favor the mother's health or life *by* taking the life of the fetus. The issue is still open, but there is no plausible prospect that Double Effect relevantly bears on its resolution.[5] It is conceivable, of course, that it could. For instance, *if* aborting the fetus at given stages was regularly possible without endangering the fetus, then, for the established practice, losing the fetus because of complications might be defended on the basis of the Principle. But where it is merely a foregone conclusion, where the causal linkage is well known, it is hopeless to pretend that the death of the fetus is not intended.

If, then, the defense of abortion is construed instrumentally, in terms of the well-being or life of the affected mother or, conceivably, in terms of the affected family, loved ones, or society, then it is impossible to avoid the question of the ethical priority of the interests or rights of the affected parties. It is in this connection that the most important and most strenuous claims are made.

The central thread of the adjusted arguments concerns the innocence of the fetus. On the most extreme antiabortion view, given the innocence of the fetus, the deliberate act of ending its life is murder.[6] The argument is that the fetus is a human being and cannot be killed *qua* innocent. As it stands, the argument is impeccable. But if so, how can abortion possibly be defended? One consideration is that the principle of innocence is, however useful, entirely vacuous, rather like the presumption of innocence in the law. One cannot defensibly take the life of an innocent being because that being is innocent: the thesis is tautological. But a defense can, in principle, be based on considerations other than innocence. Clarifying cases arise in other contexts. Imagine, for example, that a human infant or adult is affected with a deadly disease that threatens to wipe out an entire population unless the creature is dispatched. Surely it is an eligible argument to hold that the one affected ought to be killed to save the lives of the community, without denying the innocence of the victim: it is not important that the argument be decisive, only that it be eligible. For, if it is eligible, we recognize the possibility of defending the deliberate taking of another's life in spite of innocence. Hence, it is at least possible that abortion be instrumentally defended in spite of the admitted innocence of the fetus, on any non-tendentious reading of "innocence." Again, it is not normally relevant to the debate that the pregnant woman involved be anything but innocent herself, in fact as innocent as the unborn fetus. So it may very well be that the woman's rights regarding life and well-being are in some way threatened by the continued existence of the fetus, in spite of the fact that both are innocent; here, the possibility of another defense begins to take shape.

Recently, in Pennsylvania, an abortion bill that sought to specify defensible abortion solely in terms of the fetus' posing a medically confirmed danger to the very life of the mother was defeated. The

standing law, in Pennsylvania, since the bill was vetoed by the governor and not overridden, holds only that illegal abortions cannot be
legally performed. It provides no specification of what is legal or illegal
in abortion: the result is that it has been construed in the most liberal
terms possible. But the opponents of existing Pennsylvania practice
wished to reject rape and incest and the health, well-being, and mere
desires of the mother as possible grounds for justified abortion. They
do not hold that there are absolutely no grounds for defensible abortion;
there is, in fact, hardly anyone today who would deny that abortion is
justifiable if the fetus threatens the very life of the mother: the single
case of ectopic pregnancy makes this quite clear. But very few dispu-
tants pay attention to the import of the concession. What it actually
means is that the question of innocence is largely irrelevant to the
defense of abortion. For, for the usual cases, both the fetus and the
mother are innocent and their respective interests or rights, legitimate;
also, if abortion is justified or condemned, it will be, in terms of the
comparative ranking of those respective rights, without attention to
innocence, which may be presupposed. This means that the admission
of a right to abortion where the mother's life is in danger affects all
serious dispute, *so that abortion cannot be construed as murder simply
because the victim is an innocent human being*.

The thesis has larger implications. To hold that it is indefensible to
take the life of an innocent human being, whether in war, abortion,
securing public health, or the like, is open to an important equivocation. Formulated *sans phrase*, it is, as we have seen, merely tautological;
to deny it is to contradict oneself, but to admit it is not to preclude some
justifying circumstances in which innocent lives may be defensibly
taken, precisely where some suitably qualifying phrase may be supplied. Formulated *sans phrase*, innocence is merely a relevant consideration, never a decisive one. In the qualified sense, insistence on innocence is rather like an overriding verdict that cannot be set aside for any
extenuating circumstance whatsoever; so construed, an analogous
thesis would rule out even self-defense involving deliberate killing. In
the first sense, the judgment of innocence marks a consideration
bearing on an ulterior verdict, sometimes characterized as *ceteris
paribus* considerations; that is, "all things being equal," taking the lives
of innocent humans is indefensible, but whether all things are relevantly equal in this or that instance remains undecided. Now then, if, in
abortion cases, innocence is admitted for both the mother and the
fetus, and it is a *ceteris paribus* consideration, then the verdict will have
to be rendered in terms of the competing rights of the mother and
fetus. In that sense, admitting that no one holds there *never* are legiti-

mate grounds for taking the life of an innocent human being, it is simply irrelevant to charge that abortion is murder *because* the fetus is innocent. What this means is that a good many, possibly the preponderant share, of the antiabortionist arguments must be irrelevant. If, for instance, the Pennsylvania antiabortionists admit that the fetus' life may be ended to save the mother's, then they cannot, on pain of contradiction, argue that ending the fetus' life because the pregnancy involves rape or incest, or because the mother's health and well-being but not her life are endangered, is tantamount to murder simply because the fetus was an innocent human life. They have already conceded that innocence is a *ceteris paribus* consideration; only if there were no ulterior defense, as in killing a child in cold blood in the street, could the act be construed as murder; but that is precisely what is in dispute.

The argument is a conditional one. It does not count at all against the seemingly categorical argument that there never are legitimate grounds for taking an innocent life, a view perhaps espoused by Pope Pius XII: "The baby in the maternal breast has the right to life immediately from God. Hence there is no man, no human authority, no science, no medical, eugenic, social, economic or moral 'indication' which can establish or grant a valid juridical ground for a direct deliberate disposition of an innocent human life, that is a disposition which looks to its destruction either as an end or as a means to another end perhaps in itself not illicit. The baby, still not born, is a man in the same degree and for the same reason as the mother."[7] Even this formulation, however, may not be quite as extreme as it appears to be. For one thing, it may, on the equivocation specified, minimally signify that, *qua* innocent, innocent parties cannot be deliberately killed, which is benignly tautological; for another, it claims that the "right to life" proceeds from God, which is simply a doctrinally favored way of saying that we proceed, in ethical matters, from a presumption of innocence, that acts directed to taking a life call for specific ethical defense; and finally, the Pope's view may (argumentatively) be taken to signify that, with respect to abortion, appeal to the mother's health or life cannot override the right of life of the fetus, that its innocence is too powerful a consideration to be overridden by such circumstances. None of these maneuvers, singly or jointly, captures the categorical view that the taking of an innocent life is unconditionally indefensible, in the qualified sense intended.

A related equivocation infects a well-known charge of Elizabeth Anscombe's: "If someone really thinks, *in advance,* that it is open to question whether such an action as procuring the judicial execution of the innocent should be quite excluded from consideration—I do not want to argue with him; he shows a corrupt mind."[8] There is reason to think that Miss Anscombe simply does not believe that any overriding considerations would be more than implausible or fantastic, but that is not equivalent to saying that there could not, in principle, be any overriding grounds. The Pennsylvania antiabortionists, as well as antiabortionists (so-called) throughout the world, have pretty well conceded that endangering the life of the mother *is* a satisfactory reason for performing an abortion; also, we have already noted the plausibility of taking the life of a fetus—or of an infant or adult, for that matter—where the continued life of the innocent party constitutes a grave medical danger to a given community.

The reason these quarrels are important is just that they force would-be debaters to change their strategy. The consistent antiabortionist, who bases his argument on the innocence of the fetus, cannot admit endangering the mother's life as a justification for abortion; in fact, he cannot admit *any* instrumental use of abortion. And the antiabortionist who admits the danger-to-life argument cannot appeal to the innocence of the fetus as a decisive counterargument; for him, it cannot be more than a *ceteris paribus* consideration, affecting, therefore, the possibility of other instrumentalist defenses. Thus, if a human life were justifiably ended because a given creature had a disease that would destroy a population, would such a life be justifiably ended if the disease would not utterly destroy but "only" permanently and seriously disable that population? Well, if the extension be allowed, is there a sufficiently close analogy between the disease case and that of the undesirability of a fetus produced through incest or rape? Obviously, when we move on to mental health, personal well-being, desires, convictions, and the like, the arguments become increasingly tentative simply because there is no agreed-upon formula about the importance of human happiness, what form it may take, and what its prerogatives are in the scheme of things.[9]

It is impossible not to take a partisan stand on the quarrels indicated, which is not to deny the seriousness of taking a stand. But it is, also, extremely difficult to see that one *is* taking a partisan view, after all. For instance, it is often argued that "the life of the mother always prevails over the life of the unborn when both equals are in mortal conflict and she alone can be saved."[10] However persuasive it may be in these restricted circumstances, the thesis does not actually depend on the preferential ranking of the mother over the fetus but only on the prospects of exclusive survival. Certainly, we could not extrapolate from this that the mother ought always to be saved if either could be saved disjunctively; and where endangered life is not the issue, the question of ranking "the life of the mother" over "the life of the unborn" either does not arise or does so only to confirm some antecedently favored view about abortion itself. The maneuver is simply questionbegging. Again, it is often argued that "the mother and the unborn child are not like two tenants in a small house which has, by an unfortunate mistake, been rented to both: the mother *owns* the house . . . . We should really ask what it is that says no one may choose' [between mother and fetus] in the face of the fact that the body that houses the child is the mother's body."[11] But against this, there are at least two fair objections: one, we cannot speak of the fetus' body in quite the same way in which we speak of the body of an infant delivered in birth: being in the mother's body is the natural locus for a developing fetus, perhaps even some of its organs are shared with the mother or actually located, strictly enough, in the body of the mother; two, the conditions under which a woman intentionally commits herself to having a child, for instance, by contracting with her husband, may, arguably, take precedence over the "right-to-one's-body" claim.

In any case, it is an extraordinary thesis that holds that a woman's right to her body alone justifies the taking of the life of the fetus, for there is every reason to think that, even if ending the life of the fetus is sometimes justified, it need not always and unconditionally be justified—for instance, where a mother arbitrarily decides, perhaps even close to term that she simply does not want to bear her child. In short, the thesis, taken without qualification, authorizes a woman to decide in her own right whether or not, or when or perhaps even how, to dispose of the fetus "housed" in her body. The admission that the fetus has a "right to life" sets a constraint on the mother's right to her body, as do also the rights of family, loved ones, and community regarding the expected new member of a given group. For, not only is the fetus, on our assumption, a human being, but natural pregnancy, at the present time, is the exclusive means by which the race provides for its survival. This is not to favor or disfavor the alleged right of a woman to her own body, understood as justifying, at least sometimes, taking the fetus' life if her happiness, desires, or interests are seriously thwarted by its continued existence. It is to say that such a right can be construed only as a delegated right; and that whether such a delegation is a fair one or not depends on the shifting convictions of the community affected. Even if one held that a woman had a right to defend her life and a right to the use of her body, there are arguable constraints on both, bearing on the rights of others.[12] But if so, then no woman, understanding the sense of these distinctions and supposing the fetus to be a living human being, could convincingly claim to have an *un*delegated right to dispose of the fetus.

Of course, the definition of abortion is itself an ethical matter. For instance, if we treat it as a way of ending pregnancy[13] rather than as a way of ending the life of an innocent fetus, we effectively preclude the questions we have been raising. And if we consider the matter in the latter way, we are inevitably led to questions of the degree of relevant resemblance between the fetus, the human infant at birth, and fully developed human beings.[14]

We have considered the question of abortion instrumentally, in terms of the bearing of the life of the fetus on the life of the mother or on her health, well-being, happiness, and desires. And we have noted that, if an instrumental defense is allowed, we must be prepared to consider that the rights and interests of the fetus or other affected parties may, at times, take precedence over the rights and interests of the mother. For example, it may be argued that if the mother is to die shortly of causes other than pregnancy, then perhaps even if the continued pregnancy poses an additional or fatal danger, the right to life of the fetus or the rights of the father-to-be may, under the circumstances, take precedence over the woman's understandable wish to abort. These complexities cannot be eliminated and cannot be resolved in an exclusively correct way.

It is also conceivable, in certain cases at least, that abortion be defended on the grounds that the fetus is intrinsically defective or unacceptable. It is easy to see that the defense would be simplified if, in all relevant cases, the fetus were judged not to be a human being. But for reasons already given, such a maneuver would be less than interesting. The most eligible cases are, clearly, those involving extraordinary malformations, defective embryos, monsters, and, more controversially, fetuses due to rape and incest.

Here, the supporting arguments are more difficult to provide; for, if the unborn fetus, admittedly human, is innocent, has a right to life, and poses no merely instrumental threat, not even the threat of inconvenience or expense to a given community, it is hard to see what the defending grounds could be. There are, in fact, no regularized ways of speaking of cases of these sorts. For instance, where the pregnancy is due to rape or incest, it is normally the mother's prerogative to decide, in her own interests, assuming such considerations to be admissable, whether to abort or not. Nearly all forms of abortion are defended in dyadic terms, that is, instrumentally, in terms of the effects of the fetus' continued life, or of birth itself, on the interests of other human beings. Where the putative defense is construed monadically, so to say, in terms of intrinsic defects, deformities, deficiencies, or taints, we are obviously obliged to provide a theory of human nature in terms of norms of minimally acceptable physical gifts and culturally admissible conditions of conception and development. It is possible to hold, independently of the mother's wishes, that pregnancies due to incest are inherently unacceptable and must be terminated. Similarly, one can imagine a fully planned society in which all pregnancies are authorized in accord with public standards for mating or artificial insemination, by reference to which particular pregnancies are judged inadmissible or defective and abortion is required. Such a practice may need to be defended in terms of ulterior values, but particular abortions might be straightforwardly appraised in terms of a schedule of requirements. Alternatively, genetic and congenital freaks and monsters may well be judged to be sufficiently defective, *though* human, to justify abortion. In fact, there is every evidence that such abortion is regularly and quietly practiced by the medical profession, without reference to the mother's wishes or to the doctrine of innocence.

There is one other related strategy that should be mentioned. It may be argued that, in the interests of the *fetus*, it is better at times not to allow the fetus to live. For example, it may be known that a given fetus would, at birth, have permanent and crippling defects. The argument does not depend on considerations of probability, though it may be affected, as far as the interests of would-be parents are concerned, by the possibility of a subsequent, relatively normal pregnancy and by the alleged seriousness of the defects in question. It is thought to be a peculiar view because the fetus is not a rational agent, because it is not yet born, and because it is thought to be impossible to be "in the interest" of the fetus not to be born. But it is not incoherent to attribute, for instance, to future generations, interests thought to be normal or characteristic or rational for the ordinary run of men: it is simply an application of the precept of fairness to concede, to the fetus, interests no poorer or weaker than what, independently, would be conceded to fully competent and responsible adults. Thus, if suicide may be rationally undertaken, it may be entirely fair to judge it more rational to abort than to allow a seriously defective or monstrous birth. The trouble is, of course, that there is no viable way in which to *discover* the minimal conditions of acceptable fetal life; every effort merely reflects the normative convictions of given populations.[15] Hence, we must appreciate the divergence of views on abortion; within the limits of rational and responsible debate, it is entirely possible for people of conscience to disagree radically about the defensibility of the practice and of particular acts of abortion. That fact itself is as important to public policy as the particular convictions of partisans on every side. For what it shows, most forcefully, is that in ethical matters there are indisputable instances in which diametrically opposed judgments cannot be decisively confirmed and disconfirmed on neutral grounds.

Notes

1. See Jonathan Bennett, "Whatever the Consequences," *Analysis* 26(1966): 83-102; and Joseph Margolis, *Knowledge and Existence* (New York: Oxford University Press, 1972), Ch. 8. Against construing the fetus and even the newborn infant as persons, see also H. Tristram Engelhardt, Jr., "The Ontology of Abortion," *Ethics* 80(1974): 217-34; and Michael Tooley, "Abortion and Infanticide," *Philosophy and Public Affairs* 2(1972): 37-65. Engelhardt mentions some interesting complications bearing on attempts to fix personhood at conception or at later stages of fetal development: spontaneous abortion, twinning, cloning. But he fails to consider the import of obligations to fetuses by way of analogy with generally admitted obligations to future generations.

2. See Joseph Margolis, *Values and Conduct* (New York: Oxford University Press, 1971), Ch. 10.

3. See Joseph Fletcher, *Medicine and Morals* (Princeton: Princeton University Press, 1954), Ch. 3; also, Paul Ramsey, "The Morality of Abortion," in *Life or Death: Ethics and Options,* ed. Daniel H. Labby (Seattle: University of Washington Press, 1968); Glanville Williams, *The Sanctity of Life and the Criminal Law* (New York: Alfred A. Knopf, 1968); Norman St. John-Stevas, *The Right to Life* (New York: Holt, Rinehart & Winston, 1964). One of the most comprehensive, brief discussions appears in Sissela Bok, "Ethical Problems of Abortion," *The Hastings Center Studies* 2(1974): 33-52.

4. "Double Effect, Principle of," *New Catholic Encyclopedia,* Vol. 4(New York: McGraw-Hill, 1967), pp. 1020-22.

5. See the discussion in G. E. M. Anscombe, "Modern Moral Philosophy," *Philosophy* 33(1958): 1-19; Philippa Foot, "The Problem of Abortion and the Doctrine of the Double Effect," *Oxford Review* 5(1967): 5-15; Roger Wertheimer, "Understanding the Abortion Argument," *Philosophy and Public Affairs* 1(1971): 67-95; Judith Jarvis Thomson, "A Defense of Abortion," *Philosophy and Public Affairs* 1(1971): 47-66; and Bennett, "Whatever the Consequences."

6. See Bennett, "Whatever the Consequences"; Thomson, "A Defense of Abortion."

7. *Address to the Italian Catholic Society of Midwives,* quoted in John T. Noonan, Jr., ed., *The Morality of Abortion* (Cambridge: Harvard University Press, 1970). See also Daniel Callahan, "The Sanctity of Life," in *Updating Life and Death,* ed. Donald L. Cutler (Boston: Beacon Press, 1968).

8. "Modern Moral Philosophy." The point has been discussed in detail by Bennett, "Whatever the Consequences."

9. See Margolis, *Values and Conduct.*

10. Ramsey, "The Morality of Abortion."

11. Thomson, "A Defense of Abortion."

12. See Thomson, "A Defense of Abortion."

13. See Mary Anne Warren, "On the Moral and Legal Status of Abortion," *Monist* 57(1973).

14. The matter is sensitively discussed in an as yet unpublished paper, "Abortion," by Jane English.

15. See Margolis, *Values and Conduct*. See also Marya Mannes, *Last Rights* (New York: William Morrow, 1974), where verbal juggling about such distinctions as those between passive euthanasia and active mercy killing are made to *decide* the ethical defensibility of particular acts.

4

War

The most striking and obvious feature of war is the general destruction of human life on the part of people who do not know their victims personally, who profess to be opposed to wanton killing, and who nevertheless firmly believe themselves justified in the name of principles not directly construed in terms of mere personal advantage. Still, for all the confidence so often exhibited in actual wars, even where, to the eye of an unengaged observer, the alleged principles or the application of given principles seem preposterous, it is extremely difficult to say what a war is. Clearly, not all killing is thought to be unjustified; not all killing, justified or not, is an act of war; and not all acts of war are acts of killing.

In a well-known discussion, Richard Wasserstrom offers the following plausible analysis of war: first, it "is something that takes place between countries, nation-states, rather than lesser groups of individuals"; second (on Wasserstrom's view, possibly "the most essential and distinctive" characteristic), "wars almost surely involve the use of a variety of forms of violence under a claim of right," perhaps, as a minimally necessary condition, the use of specialized functionaries, a soldiery "*prepared to kill* the soldiers of the opposing army"; third, wars are either "a circumscribed, clearly definable instrument of foreign policy" or "some indeterminate, indefinable, and unlimited fight or struggle between countries."[1] Wasserstrom's analysis quite naturally allows for some accommodation of borderline cases, for example, civil wars and the sort of private wars that have taken place in China; but it disallows such secondary or metaphorical wars as those against poverty and disease.

The trouble is that it is a conventional view and, consequently, fails to provide a proper place for unconventional but increasingly important instances of war. For example, there is every reason to think that the kind of war the radical Arab guerrilla groups have waged against the Israelis—not, be it noted, the deliberate engagements of countries like Egypt and Syria—cannot be specified in terms of the foreign policy of nation-states or suitable surrogates but only in terms of the convictions of an ethnically and religiously cohesive population and in terms, somewhat less comprehensively, of geographical unity of some sort. Again, there is every reason to believe that radical black groups in the United States, particularly those closely associated with the Black Muslim movement or those inspired by Frantz Fanon, have supposed themselves to be in an incipient state of war against the Establishment and have contemplated continuous, violent guerrilla activities as either useful to their cause or unavoidable; such activity has been muted by attacks on the headquarters of the Black Panthers and by the general stiffening of the forces of public law and order in the country, but the conception of such war could not be subsumed under Wasserstrom's formula. Also, the Marxist view of class warfare, historically developed in opposition to admitting the legitimacy of wars between states and only latterly skewed in the interest of so-called wars of national liberation, cannot be adequately characterized in terms of wars between states or even of merely civil wars. In this connection, the French Revolution, the Russian Revolution, the Chinese Revolution, even the American Revolution, which could not actually be called a class war, cannot be subsumed under the formula given. Finally, if one admits criminal organizations of such sweep as the Mafia or the Cosa Nostra, it is easy to see that a sustained and articulated war may obtain in a context in which national boundaries, though strategically relevant, do not serve to define the very form of the war at hand. The charge that cases of these sorts are either secondary or metaphorical seems tendentious or naive; and the claim that they are subsumable as instances of wars between states, possibly with minor adjustments in our conception, is simply mistaken. It is not helpful, it may be noticed, to disqualify violent revolution as a true form of war, since there is no reason to think that revolution must be confined within a "country" or a "nation-state," or that it will fail to gather armies prepared to kill "under a claim of right," or that opposing sides will not seek allies and military supplies among other powers. The same holds for other seemingly marginal forms of warfare, for instance, ethnic and racial warfare. Of course, if contests of power are, say, primarily economic and characteristically lack any form of sustained violence and killing, we may reasonably withhold the ascription of war; although, bearing in mind a larger issue, there can be no doubt that the outbreak of relevant forms of violence is noticeably continuous with certain political and economic struggles typically said to obtain under conditions of peace.

The reason the quarrel is important is that one of the most desperately pressing questions of the day asks whether and when war may be morally justified; any answer presupposes that the phenomenon of war may be conceptually segregated in a fairminded way. But *if* the Arab guerrilla killing of Israeli athletes at the 1972 Olympics was a bona fide act of war, then, now that the guerrillas are out of Germany and will never be extradited, the complication of local jurisdiction, in terms of which the Arabs would have been tried for murder, need not affect our reflections on the legitimacy of what they did; on the other hand, if we adhere to the conventional view of war, say, Wasserstrom's, then there is no possibility of attempting to justify their act as an act of war. Since, presumably, that is their own view of the matter, it seems tendentious to disallow it in order to remain consistent with Wasserstrom's formula. Of course, it is reasonably clear that the guerrillas' action could not be justified as an instance of conventional warfare.

All the vexed questions about the justification of war and the justification of killing in war depend on how we manage this definitional issue. For instance, it is stalwartly maintained by Elizabeth Anscombe, speaking of war in the context of Catholic conviction, though not as a sectarian, that "the deliberate choice of inflicting death in a struggle is the right only of ruling authorities and their subordinates."[2] There are constraints regarding innocence that Miss Anscombe holds qualify the precept given, but they need not concern us for the moment. Verbal quibbles, conceivably, might allow us to claim, consistently with the thesis, that an unjust authority is a contradiction in terms and that such putative authorities do not actually rule. The debatable, even chaotic possibilities of such a reading are perfectly obvious. Even so, for the counterinstances proposed, there is no way to specify a "ruling authority" uncontroversially. In revolutionary and ethnic wars, for example, the very concept of a ruling authority must be somewhat metaphorical; and yet, it would be widely maintained that inflicting death in such circumstances was justified.

The point is that the very effort to define war, with a view to distinguishing it from merely organized killing or murder or banditry or the like, is nothing but a strategy sought by potential parties to wars of a certain form, who understand that the security, orderliness, and predictability of their own favored form of conflict are jeopardized by admitting the radical variety of war, its changeability with regard to fundamentals, and the prospect that the old order of things may be challenged or even eclipsed by an emerging order. These possibilities were certainly felt with the advent, say, of Marxist criticism and, more particularly, with the rise of palpable forces committed to the concept of class warfare. Again, it is entirely possible, in America, for instance, that the polarization of the races may shape a compelling ideology of prolonged racial war, the existence of which could be confirmed by the appearance of pitched battles in the cities or at least sustained guerrilla activity and all that that entails.

There is only one effective basis for avoiding the conclusion suggested, namely that, in some sense, the moral norms essential to human nature can be discovered *and* that political life of every possible sort, including war, may be judged in terms of those norms. The first consideration bears on providing independent cognitive grounds for normative constraints on behavior in general;[3] the second, the prospect of specifically applying such distinctions to the conduct of war. The first is not as such the issue of relativism: it is not a question of convergence among competing moral doctrines; it is a question of whether putative moral constraints can be shown to be defensible on cognitive grounds. The second obliges us to consider more closely the conceptual peculiarities of war itself, particularly, the features of whatever entities are said to engage in war.

Realistically, it is inconceivable that all parties to armed conflict would be able to agree with Miss Anscombe's substantive judgments about just and unjust wars, though they might, each from his own vantage, appear to agree that "there [is] such a thing as the common good of mankind" and that we can discern "an objectively unjust proceeding." It is by reason of such a belief that Miss Anscombe is prepared to rely on the "right of ruling authorities," even when they themselves are parties to a dispute or war. The only other basis for avoiding a skeptical conclusion depends on the belief that warring parties somehow come to agree, perhaps by way of a common tradition, about the very rules of the game of war. This is surely the officers' view in Erich von Stroheim's *Grand Illusion,* possibly even in a muddled way the view of Clausewitz. But it is unworkable where the forms of war already mentioned are in play. What violates the rules of comradely professional armies of World War I vintage may well be admissible in the context of contemporary racial and ethnic war; or, at any rate, it cannot be easily disqualified on the basis of anything like a formal agreement. There is nothing like a Geneva Convention for modern guerrilla warfare, even though such warfare is not, as Wasserstrom supposes, "indeterminate, indefinable, and unlimited" fighting between countries.

One of the favorite issues that the genteel discussion of war has insisted on concerns the treatment of innocent parties. Miss Anscombe, registering the prevailing view, says that it is murderous to attack innocent people. The difficulty with this pronouncement is not that it is open to telling counterinstances but that it is vacuously true.[4] She also says that "innocence is a legal notion,"[5] but if it is, then apart from appeal to a higher law, the very idea of an innocent party will be controlled by the overriding conception of how to justify a given war. For example, in a racial or ethnic war or even in a more conventional war between states that is expected to run for generations, there is no clear sense in which, say, bearing children, the future warriors of the enemy power, can be irresistibly discounted as the activity of noncombatants. What is true of women and children in this regard is true, *a fortiori,* of factory workers, Red Cross personnel, priests, and the like.

Constraints on attacking this or that fraction of an enemy population depend at least on the clarity with which a distinctly professionalized army may be specified: talk about the people's militia, treat every infant as a budding soldier, organize the farmers as the nation's fighting force, and you will have blurred the very basis on which the older distinction between combatant and non-combatant was drawn. That the United States had difficulty enlisting public support for bombing the North Vietnamese countryside is a concession to culture lag, not to the persistence of an independently and indisputably defensible doctrine. At any rate, in the face of novel forms of war and of the apparently sincere rejection of constraints that, in more conventional wars, were thought to bind the behavior of combatants, it is difficult to see that the old constraints can be merely assumed to be fair. What is the reason for thinking that newer views about what is admissible in newer wars and newer kinds of war ought to conform to what, in an earlier time, was taken for granted?

But the point about innocence and the demarcation of combatants forces us to pay attention to a much more profound difficulty in all the humane talk about confining war within moral boundaries. Wasserstrom was in a way right in linking war to the foreign policy of national states, not in what he explicitly says but, so to say, about the kind of linkage between war and human societies. For war need not be an instrument of *foreign* policy; it needs only to be construed as an instrument of *external* policy. And, it need not be an instrument of *national states*; it needs only to be construed as an instrument of *collective entities*. The war between the Palestinian guerrillas and the Kingdom of Jordan, which ended so disastrously for the guerrillas, cannot possibly be viewed as concerned with foreign relations; but it was concerned with external relations between two collective bodies, Jordan as a conventional national state and the guerrillas as a distinct people within the geographical boundaries of that state. The concept of foreign relations does not provide for the distinction of relevant entities where no conventional geographic divisions can be supplied.

Here, we must be as hardheaded as we can. On an economical view of what there is in the world, collective entities—states, nations, corporations, clans, socioeconomic classes, societies—do not exist as such; only individual human beings exist, whose beliefs, behavior, objectives, and the like may be directed to the alleged interests of such collective entities. Biologically, only human beings exist and have interests; but, given their training as competent agents, they divide their energies spontaneously between their own interests and the doctrinally projected "interests" of purely fictitious, but not for that reason unimportant, entities. Nations, so to say, "have interests" only because aggregates of human beings interpret their *own* behavior as serving the national interest. The reason this is crucial is quite straightforward: *war is an instrument of external policy on the part of a collective entity, but collective entities do not exist.* The demarcation between combatants and non-combatants, that is, between distinct aggregates of individuals, cannot, therefore, but be a distinction of a secondary sort. War is not fought against individual men but against collective entities, though only individuals fight. The conception that we are engaged in war entails that we are in some sense agents of an ideologically specified entity, whose "interests" and "activities" are of principal concern and are ranged against those of other collective entities. In the case of civil war, where the rebels construe the internal relations of some "legitimate" entity as external relations between distinct powers, we have what may be termed a logically degenerate instance of war.

Of course, the thesis is arguable. But *if* it can be sustained, the distinction between combatants and non-combatants and the justification of waging war in the interests of a given nation, socioeconomic class, ethnic community, or the like cannot but be the expression of the very ideologies by which those entities are thought to exist.

People act. They do so singly or in aggregations, that is, aggregatively—cooperatively, competitively, congruently. To talk of collective action is to risk equivocation: to act collectively, as in marching, is merely to act aggregatively; but it may be held, by way of ideology, that to act collectively signifies that a *collective entity acts* and that the actions of individual people are merely the events that embody the action of a collective entity. The United States declared war on Japan, for instance, but it did so through the speech of President Roosevelt. When the requisite doctrines are embedded in the habits of given aggregates, people spontaneously refer and commit their energies to the "interests" and "objectives" of such entities. But, unless we adopt the so-called idealist theory of the organic state or the so-called materialist theory about the existential priority of socioeconomic classes over human individuals, it is not literally true that collective entities *exist,* *have* interests, and *act.*

The point is central to the argument and cannot be softened. Collective entities are merely intentional objects, that is, "objects" that need not exist in order that the appropriate activities obtain. For instance, we say that a man *serves his country* in war. But he may do so if he only believes that his country is an actual entity whose proper interests, not to be confused with his own, he serves: he serves his country in the same sense in which Ponce de Leon sought the Fountain of Youth.

The reason collective entities are fictional is just that we can only *imagine* them to *have* interests or to *commit* acts.[6] Nothing can act or have an interest that is not at the very least sentient or intelligent. Human beings, singly and aggregatively, satisfy these conditions. A corporation, for instance, can only have interests imputed to it. The argument is that simple. But to say this much is not to deny that people believe, or act as if they believe, that collective entities actually exist; nor is it to deny that human aggregates are really caught up in relationships that have a distinctly collective import. To say that there is no such *entity* as a socioeconomic class, in the sense in which a class is said to have its own interests, is not to deny that we enter into class *relationships* or to deny that we may justifiably claim that this or that serves, say, the interests of the capitalist class.

Still, war is an instrument of external policy on the part of collective (intentional) entities. So it is impossible to separate the appraisal of war from the admission of the fictitious entities that engage in war; and it is impossible to acknowledge such entities without subscribing to the ideologies that say they exist. The admission of war entails the admission of collective entities. Deny reference to such entities and we must reinterpret the phenomenon of war itself. Change the conception of what entities collect our allegiance and we risk changing our convictions about their conduct in war.

It is in this sense that other well-known problems are rendered more difficult than they are ordinarily thought to be. For example, modern technological warfare, which cannot readily confine destruction to pinpointed targets, not only threatens to make a shambles of every distinction between combatants and non-combatants but threatens to make utterly inoperative any distinction between intended and merely foreseen consequences; that is, the distinction covered by the Principle of Double Effect. [7] It is simply naive to insist that, in war, human combatants have no right to inflict death and harm on these or those innocent parties; for that entails that one's own ideology properly designates who and whose behavior embody the combatant interests and conduct of the hostile *collective* entity. And it is equally naive to insist that a fair line can be drawn between the intended and the merely foreseen consequences for some *aggregated* population; for that entails that one's ideology properly specifies how the effects of war on given *aggregates* embody defensible effects on the *collective* entities that are actually at war. The same issue arises in the difficult matter of war crimes and the responsibility of functioning agents of the state to obey superior orders—say, men and officers in an army, or clerks and guards in a concentration camp—when the actions of individual men are said to constitute crimes against humanity. [8] For, apart from the issue of so-called victors' trials, Nuremburg, for instance, and apart from the pragmatic difficulties of avoiding or resisting superior orders during wartime, regardless of one's conscience, there remains the conceptual difficulty of justifying imposing one set of ideological constraints on what is admissible under an alternative doctrine.

The point is that the usual humane criticism of killing the innocent, of technological warfare, of persons committing horrid acts in the name of their war duties normally fails to address itself to the conceptual question of the grounds on which the acts of collective entities may be justifiably constrained or censured or resisted as by war, or the grounds on which responsibility for those acts may be distributed to aggregates of persons whose own individual acts embody but are not the same as the former. It is a conceptual oversight that conflates the question of assigning individual responsibility or liability, given collective responsibility, with the question of assigning individual responsibility or liability, given aggregative responsibility. In the first instance, the conduct of individuals is taken to *embody* the "conduct" of collective entities, in accord with a favored ideology; in the second, the conduct of aggregates is a *summation* of some sort of the determinate conduct of individuals, in accord with various parameters. There will, obviously, be competing principles on which the assignment of responsibility will be defended in either context; nevertheless, there is no simple or neutral way to reduce assignments of the first sort to assignments of the second. As a matter of fact, a related confusion appears in utilitarian arguments that advocate sacrificing values serving individuals or particular aggregates for the sake of what serves "the greatest good for the greatest number"; but it is hardly confined to utilitarianism.[9]

Furthermore, it is of decisive importance whether, in judging the behavior of individual combatants, appraisal is internal to the ideology in question or externally applied by way of an alien ideology or some allegedly independent principle. In the first case, the issue only concerns consistency vis-à-vis given rules; in the second, an ulterior question arises as to how to justify objectively the behavioral norms of *any* collective entity. Presumably, as in charging crimes against humanity, the argument obliges us to show how the activities of collective entities legitimately further the proper ideals of human beings. And that entails the provision of norms essential to human nature, for which there is not the slightest prospect of confirmation.[10] Also, in the absence of any such discovery, the competing ideologies will generate their own favored claims about what ought to govern our behavior. So it is practically impossible to break through the circle of competing ideologies. In fact, if it could be done, then, rationally, either there would be no need for collective entities with their competing values or else they would be no more than social instruments by which to abbreviate, in practice, our commitments regarding the entire human population.

With these distinctions in mind, we may say, fairly, that the argument is doubly conditional. For one thing, it needs to be shown that there are or are no cognitive grounds by which to discover the correct norms of personal behavior. And for a second, it needs to be shown how, if war is the work of collective entities, it is possible to provide objective grounds for constraining *such* entities and human beings insofar as they act as their agents. We have explored the second condition primarily, allowing the first to stand as an unsupported assumption;[11] for, if collective entities are fictitious despite their being

the putative agents of war, it seems impossible to provide a corresponding account about the "conduct" of collective entities.

Consider, now, the details of censuring the behavior of individual
persons acting as the agents of states at war, as in the My Lai massacre
or the Eichmann atrocities. There is, first of all, the purely internal
question whether the acts of given individuals were authorized or fell,
as a discretionary option, within some authorization. If there is no
sense in which they were thus authorized, then they could not have
been the acts of warring agents, or of warring agents acting in their
capacity as such, but only of individuals contingently involved in war.
The man who takes his neighbor's life under cover of an enemy attack
is guilty of a crime but not for waging war criminally. The charges
against Lieutenant Calley and Rudolf Eichmann, however, explicitly
concern the criminal status of what they did as agents fulfilling their
duties in prosecuting the war. Furthermore, Calley and Eichmann
were judged criminally liable, respectively, by an internal and an
external judicial review. However fair we may suppose Eichmann's
trial to have been, the man was judged in accord with the Israeli
conception of the duties of agents or in accord with higher obligations
that putatively take precedence over duties authorized by any state.
The point is worth pressing, because, if such higher obligations were
genuinely objective, then the entailed criticism could not have been
merely external to the Eichmann case, even if managed through an
external court (that is just the point of speaking of "crimes against
humanity"); but *if* such obligations could not be objective in the sense
required, the charge that Eichmann pursued his war duties criminally
must be nothing but the intrusion of an alternative inimical ideology.

The point may be put more compendiously. If we think of war
crimes, we think of individual men or aggregates as agents of collective
entities: their responsibilities must be construed in terms of superior
orders or in the initiation of orders to be followed. Internally, the only
question that arises is conformity with such orders or the consistency
of such orders relative to the ideology of the power involved or the
responsibility of superiors for the conduct of those under their command; externally, counterpart questions may be raised in accord with
the ideology of the reviewing power. The cases of Lieutenant Calley
and General Yamashita exhibit the quarrelsome nature of such
review.[12] If, however, we wish to avoid tendentiousness, we may
attempt to construe war crimes committed by individuals as falling
under the laws or traditions of a competent state or the like, where the
war context is not essential. We may also attempt to construe crimes
committed during war, even if in accord with superior orders, as

"crimes against humanity." In this sense, it is sometimes said that Calley was guilty of massacre, without justification of any sort;[13] and it is said that the defendants at Nuremburg violated the implied constraints that "humanity" imposes on all forms of war.[14] The trouble is that the very concept of war entails that justification for the wholesale destruction of life and property is *debatable*. Hence, it is impossible that the conduct of agents in war can be satisfactorily reduced, for purposes of moral or legal review, to whatever falls under the "normal" rules of admissible conduct where war does not obtain; and it is impossible that the constraints the interests of humanity are said to impose on war and conduct during war could escape being ideologically captured, once it is admitted that the wholesale destruction of life and property is, in principle, compatible with such constraints. The outrageousness of Calley's behavior and of Eichmann's actually obscures the conceptual issue of the relationship between acting in accord with superior orders and the alleged constraints of the "rules of war" and the "interests of humanity." The concept of "military necessity," for example, tends to favor any course of action reasonably required for victory;[15] crimes against peace and humanity tend to reflect competing ideological convictions; and distinctions between combatant and non-combatant and intended and foreseen consequences are, as we have seen, inevitably tendentious.

Now, what is true of the acts of the agents of collective entities is even more obviously true of the "acts" of those collective entities themselves. Individual men cannot wage war except *as* agents of collective entities at war. But the political and moral ideals of collective entities cannot be challenged by the "beliefs" and "interests" of other collective entities, except on a partisan basis; and where the policy and practice of a collective entity is judged or censured by individual men, presumably not as partisans of some ideology, there is no other basis for appraisal that moral consensus or the alleged discovery of the natural norms of human behavior. Given familiar ideological conflicts, however, there cannot be a realistic expectation of consensus, except perhaps within a range of congruent ideologies. Is there any reason to think, for instance, that the killing of the Israeli athletes in the 1972 Olympics was not sincerely viewed, on the part of the guerrillas, as a justified act of war in a just war? Or, that the technique of gradual starvation used by the Nigerians against the Biafrans, notably effective against children, was not, under the circumstances, viewed as a justified act of war in a just war? Or, that the Soviets' crushing of the Hungarian uprising was not viewed as a justified act of war in a just (however brief) war? Or, that the American bombing of Hanoi and

Haiphong was not viewed as a justified act of war in a just (however undeclared) war? Or, that the Chinese annexation of Tibet was not viewed as a justified act of war in a just (however improbable) war?

This is not, of course, to concede every ideological conviction as self-validating or to deny the possibility of rational grounds for the censure or justification of war, particular wars, or of particular acts committed in pursuing a war. But it is to emphasize that there is no ready moral consensus about war conduct that is not itself substantially the reflection of conventional views; also, that the usual appraisals completely neglect the dialectical relationship between the "acts" of states and the acts of individual persons.

There is a further complication. Even if it is conceded that international instruments governing the conduct of war have been formulated and agreed to by participating *states*, for instance, as in the Geneva Convention or the Kellogg-Briand Pact, such instruments presuppose the legitimacy of the participating powers; the powers themselves are constrained only within the limits of their agreement; non-signatory powers are not bound by the agreement; and the signatory powers have no relevant means of appraising the alternative practices and policies of non-signatory powers, particularly those organized in accord with entirely different principles and ideals, except in terms of their own converging ideologies. Even admitting the repugnant and irrational nature of Hitler's general claims, was the ceding of the Sudeten territory to Germany justified or utterly unjustified and would Germany have been justified, on being refused at that point, in going to war with Czechoslovakia? Or, given the Soviet version of the Marxist ideology, was the crushing of the Dubček Spring justified? If Jordan were prepared to make a separate peace with Israel, would Syria be justified in invading Jordan, in order to forestall the failure of a putatively just and larger cause? Given the North Vietnamese picture of American aggression in Southeast Asia, were the North Vietnamese justified in invading the apparently sovereign territories of Laos and Cambodia?

The admission of collective entities depends, as we have seen, on the habits of mind of aggregates of men. Viewed internally, the state provides the political context within which the preferred political and non-political values of some aggregate are most effectively pursued. Being a fiction in the sense supplied, collective entities cannot but be committed to their own survival and to the maintenance or enlargement of their power; only in that way, on the interpretation of any ideology that admits competing powers, could they "act" to achieve or make accessible the objectives of their home population. Even the

Marxist "withering away of the state" presupposes the intervening agency of the proletariat as a collective entity and is to obtain only in the limit when class differences are effectively erased.

So there is no clear demarcation, internally, between the prudential and the moral or political objectives of given collective entities. External insistence on demarcation is simply the expression of an alien and non-converging ideology; an internal admission is simply the expression of a provisional ranking of a collective entity's own priorities. In any event, we must not confuse the constraints a collective entity "imposes" on itself and the constraints human aggregates impose on themselves and on such entities. When human aggregates risk the "survival" of the state in the name of allegedly higher values as in civil war and revolution, they correspondingly change those habits of mind on the basis of which alone the state effectively "exists"; also, characteristically, as in civil war and revolution, they expect to constitute a new state in place of the old and to shift their loyalties. This is the point of the separatist movements of Bangaladesh, Northern Ireland, Biafra, South Vietnam, the Kurds, the Croatians, the Ukrainians, and the Black Muslims, as well as the deeper upheavals of the French and Russian Revolutions. Viewed externally by other effective collective entities, given states or surrogates must be viewed prudentially, that is, as impinging on the policies and practices of a particular entity and as committed or not to compatible objectives.

In a sense, these considerations vindicate Hobbes' well-known thesis that political states are in a state of nature, that is, a state of war vis-à-vis one another. *Given* their ideologies and overriding values, collective entities see themselves threatened by the existence and commitment of every other such entity. Political states are not viewed, internally, as mere instruments for securing certain values; they are viewed essentially as providing the very system of life in which given values may be embodied. Individuals, of course, may construe political states instrumentally. But to make their appraisals convincing, they require an independent, objective moral principle by which to constrain collective entities as such and to appraise relations that hold between individuals and such entities; and that, as has been argued, seems most unpromising to defend.

Effectively, then, human beings judge the behavior of their own states and other states in terms of their own loyalties. It is quite likely that, attempting to justify their allegience on independent, rational grounds, individual human beings would be utterly baffled; but the problem does not arise for people who already regard themselves as member parts of such entities. The point of Hobbes' thesis, that indi-

viduals in a state of nature—outside all political organization—are in a
state of war "of all against all," is clear enough. But Hobbes' use of the
term "war" to characterize the behavior of individual persons as well
as of collective entities and his failure to distinguish carefully between
the behavior of aggregates and collective entities obscure the conceptual relations involved. We may, perhaps, restrict the use of "war" to
distinctly violent behavior of a certain sort. But if there is no independent basis for discerning normative constraints on political behavior,
then, in politics as in morals, the best that human beings can do is to act
as rational and informed partisans. And then, in the Hobbesian sense,
aggregates of human beings, acting as political agents, are in a state of
war against one another, in that the states to which they are loyal are in
a state of war.

The critical issue, then, is that war is properly ascribed to collective
entities, not to individual persons or to aggregates, except deriva-
tively. Collective entities "exist" in the sense in which they are the
intentional objects of sustained human endeavor not otherwise relevantly characterized. The difficulties involving the responsibility of
agents in war does not actually require that collective entities be fictions: the distribution of aggregative responsibility is complex
enough. That states are fictions depends on considerations regarding
the ascription of personal attributes to putative entities that lack brains
and minds; and their being fictions affects the very possibility of a
cognitive basis for constraining "their" behavior. It also dramatizes, of
course, the hypnotic power of ideologies, in virtue of which individuals spontaneously direct their own activities to the interests and objectives of such entities. What has been stressed here is the sense in
which, apart from formal constraints of coherence, relevance, and
avoidance of arbitrariness, the justification of war and the justification
of the conduct of aggregates in war are essentially inseparable from
matters of ideological conviction. Given policies may be shown to be indefensible on formal or dialectical grounds; but the positive justification
of such policies cannot be freed from some governing ideology. For
instance, it is sometimes argued that it is morally indefensible to
pursue a war that is known with certainty to be impossible not to lose.
But this would mean that the Finns were wrong to prosecute their war
against the Russians; or that Indian tribes were wrong to war against
the whites; or that Poland was wrong to war against the Nazis. As a
matter of fact, the defeat of a collective entity may entail all sorts of
relative gains for that entity and for the aggregates that compose it; in
any case, the thesis fails to attend carefully enough to the difference
between the condition of a collective entity and the condition of human

aggregates. Again, it is sometimes argued that it is morally indefensible to pursue a war at any price.[16] But if war itself is ideologically justified and entails wholesale slaughter, it cannot but be an ideological gambit that holds that the price is too high. To block the conclusion, we should have to show that the proper norms of human conduct are determinate and discernible; that collective entities are actually existent; and natural norms, assignable to them. But if the countermoves fail, the very designation of conflicts *as* wars, rather than as insurrections, revolts, civil disturbances, palace coups, police actions, anarchy, is itself an instrument *of* war.

Notes

1. Richard Wasserstrom, "On the Morality of War," *Stanford Law Review* 21(1969): 1627-56. See also L. Oppenheim, *International Law,* ed. H. Lauterpacht (New York: Longmans, Green, 1952), Vol. II, Part 2, Ch. 1.

2. G. E. M. Anscombe, "War and Murder," in *Nuclear Weapons: A Catholic Response,* ed. Walter Stein (New York: Sheed and Ward, 1961).

3. See Joseph Margolis, *Values and Conduct* (New York: Oxford University Press, 1971).

4. Anscombe, "War and Murder." See also, John Ford, "The Morality of Obliteration Bombing," *Theological Studies* 5(1944): 261-309.

5. Anscombe, "War and Murder."

6. There is an ulterior question concerning reference to fictional and intentional entities and concerning what there is or exists. For a sustained discussion, see Joseph Margolis, *Knowledge and Existence* (New York: Oxford University Press, 1973), Ch. 4.

7. "Double Effect, Principle of," *New Catholic Encyclopedia,* Vol. 4 (New York: McGraw-Hill, 1967), pp. 1020-22. See also Anscombe, "War and Murder," and Ford, "The Morality of Obliteration Bombing."

8. See the well-documented study by G. Lewy, "Superior Orders, Nuclear Warfare, and the Dictates of Conscience: The Dilemma of Military Obedience in the Atomic Age," *American Political Science Review* 55(1961): 3-23.

9. Stuart Hampshire, "Morality and Pessimism," *The New York Review of Books,* 25 January 1973, pp. 26-33.

10. See Margolis, *Values and Conduct,* Chs. 4-5.

11. But see Margolis, *Values and Conduct* for a sustained discussion of the prospects of a cognitive basis for discerning the normative values binding on human beings.

12. The most quoted review of the issues is provided in Telford Taylor, *Nuremberg and Vietnam: An American Tragedy* (Chicago: Quadrangle Books, 1970). See also Peter A. French, ed., *Individual and Collective Responsibility: Massacre at My Lai* (Cambridge: Schenckman, 1972).

13. For example, see Virginia Held, "Moral Responsibility and Collective Action," in French, *Individual and Collective Responsibility.*

14. For example, see Marshall Cohen, "Morality and the Laws of War," in Virginia Held et al., eds., *Philosophy, Morality, and International Affairs* (New York: Oxford University Press, 1974).

15. For example, see R. B. Brandt, "Utilitarianism and the Rules of War," *Philosophy and Public Affairs* 1(1972): 145-65; and Richard Wasserstrom, "The Legal Responsibility of the Individual for War Crimes," in Held, *Individual and Collective Responsibility;* also, Richard Wasserstrom, "The Laws of War," *The Monist* 56(1972).

16. These putatively moral rules were advanced, for instance, by Alasdair MacIntyre and Arthur Danto, at the Conference on Morality and International Violence, Kean College of New Jersey, April 22-24, 1974. Again, in the same Conference, R.M. Hare held that terrorism could not be morally justified because either it could not be "universalized" or because it could only be "fanatically" universalized; but that view entails converting a non-moral consideration of consistency of usage into a morally effective criterion or intruding a tendentious reading of "fanatical." Once wars are admitted to be not necessarily fanatical, terrorism must be as well: also, of course, to characterize activities as "terrorist" is to link them, favorably or unfavorably, to certain ideological views of the objectives pursued.

5

Crime

The embarrassment of penal institutions lies with their general ineffectiveness in reducing recidivism and reforming or rehabilitating criminals, the expense and seeming barbarity of large institutions designed essentially to inflict pain and hardship on convicted criminals with little or no prospect of redeeming benefit, and the positive contribution of jails and penitentiaries to criminal expertise and criminal propensities. Penal reformers tend to think of criminals as victimized somehow by their own biology, their social and economic circumstances, and their psychological confusions. So viewed, crime should be eliminable by the enlightened reform of institutions, the improvement of the rehabilitative function of punishment and of therapeutic or other alternatives to punishment, and the gradual elimination, by breeding, of those found to be biologically disposed to criminal behavior.[1] No doubt there is *something* to be said favoring all such theories, assuming the relevant causal claims can be confirmed, which, at the present time, is not an altogether promising prospect.[2] The main difficulty rests with the concept of crime itself. Thus, for instance, in a strongly skeptical vein, Austin Turk categorically states that "efforts to determine causes of criminality have foundered on the fact that criminality is not a biological, psychological, or even behavioral phenomenon, but a social status defined by the way in which an individual is perceived, evaluated, and treated by legal authorities."[3] Turk favors the prominent view that "criminality is . . . the state of having been officially defined as *punishable,* whether or not one has been apprehended and *punished"*; but he also stresses its inadequacy where the concept of punishment is not suitably constrained by attention to differences between criminal and civil law and between criminal law and conventional morality.[4] He adds: "there is apparently no pattern of human behavior which has not been at least tolerated in some normative structure," and, "the behavioral elements comprising an illegal act are not specific to criminal as distinguished from other human behavior."[5]

It seems that the empirical evidence favors a positivist view of criminality: criminals are those and only those judged, by those authorized to judge, to have violated the criminal law. But the positivist view holds as well that the law is an instrument of coercion resting on ethical norms that, for conceptual reasons, cannot be demonstrated or simply enacted into law but only presupposed.[6] The point is a crucial one. For, if crime were a deviation from natural norms discoverable by an exercise of science or reason, then in explaining the causes of relevantly deviant behavior we should be explaining the causes of crime and criminality. As it is, lacking such an account, even though whatever contingently counts as criminal may be causally explained, we should not have touched at all on the explanation of crime as such. Crime, as Turk insists, is a kind of *status* assigned to our behavior; and criminality is merely the state of having that status assigned, not in any other sense a determinate feature of our actual behavior. There can be no pertinent causal accounts of evaluative appraisals, though what they concern—behavior, in the case of crime—has a causal history.

The positivist tradition is defective, however, because it fails to pursue the question of the relationship between law and morality beyond the admission that ethical norms are presupposed. Hans Kelsen corrects an extreme and primitive positivism by admitting that ethical norms *are embodied* in the law, but his own positivist scruples forbid him to attempt any justification.[7] Clearly, where liability to punishment is entailed, particularly with regard to criminal law, the issue cannot be avoided. Even on internal grounds, the admission that legal norms embody ethical norms threatens the plausibility of any thesis that restricts analysis to the "actual law," the law as it putatively is. The distinction between a purely internal and a purely external review of the law cannot but be blurred by efforts to resolve contradictory laws or contradictory interpretations of the law, or to demonstrate that there are no gaps in the law or to provide laws where there are gaps, or to determine the proper interpretation or application of the law, or to judge that laws have or have not actually issued from the legal sovereign or have or have not actually been promulgated.[8]

On the other hand, the thesis that there is a divinely revealed moral law by which positive law may be correctly appraised, a thesis shared, historically, by Catholics, Protestants, Jews, and Muslims, is simply inadmissible in any fair attempt to justify criminal law on rational grounds. The thesis that there is a natural law, congruent with divine law, that men may penetrate by the use of reason alone, is, apart from the conceptual difficulties of its defense, rendered utterly useless by the more or less frank admissions of its stoutest advocates. Norman St. John-Stevas, for example, acknowledges that "in many controverted moral problems . . . the natural law does not provide a certain guide." He treats this as "a practical difficulty" since, though "the distinction between natural law and divine law is sharp in theory, . . . in practice . . . individuals employing their reason reach diametrically opposed conclusions about natural law rules." He cites, favorably, Pius XII's encyclical *Humani Generis*, which simply says, observing "that man's senses, imagination, and evil passions hinder him from grasping truths that transcend the sensible order,"

> It is for this reason that divine revelation must be called morally necessary, so that those religious and moral truths, which are not of their nature beyond the reach of reason may, also in the present condition of the human race be known by all with ease, with unwavering certitude, and without any admixture of error.[9]

Naively put, whatever harms an individual or society is liable to be judged criminal. Hence, criminal law and law in general cannot be autonomous: whatever procedural autonomy it may be accorded must be premised on some theoretical connection between its operative norms and the ulterior concerns, including the moral concerns, of the society in which they obtain. The natural law tradition, which provides an obvious connection between law and morality, is opposed by the prevailing tradition of secular positive law.[10] In any case, the complications regarding determinate positive law cannot be readily resolved within the natural law tradition. On the other hand, its definition of law, which does capture the conceptual connection between law and morality, neatly exposes the inadequacy of the positivist view itself. Law, says St. Thomas, is

> an ordinance of reason for the common good, made by him who has care of the community and has promulgated [it].[11]

Leaving questions of legal sovereignty and the details of determinate positive law aside, it is reasonably clear that every formulation of the nature of criminal law must conform to this general definition. Thus, both H.L.A. Hart, who, in effect, dismisses appeals to natural law in legal and metalegal disputes, and St. John-Stevas, who accepts the natural law argument but endorses a sensitivity to its "practical" inadequacies, favorably cite the Wolfenden Committee's (partial) definition of criminal law (formulated primarily and originally to cover sexual matters):

> [The] function [of the criminal law], as we see it, is to preserve public order and decency, to protect the citizen from what is offensive or injurious and to provide sufficient safeguards against exploitation or corruption of others, particularly those who are specially vulnerable because they are young, weak in body or mind or inexperienced . . . .[12]

Hart construes the statement as agreeing with Mill's in *On Liberty*, which is just to say that the law, criminal law in particular, cannot justifiably be made to enforce "morality as such."[13]

Obviously, that use of the criminal law, usually applied to sexual conduct, the taking of life (one's own or another's), respect for property and person, and alleged conspiracies affecting such matters, cannot but be arbitrary or relative, without some reasoned defense of the moral norms involved. The mere variety of relevant social practices, as well as the conceptual difficulty of defending particular views on such topics as homosexuality, prostitution, polygamy, suicide, euthanasia, and pornography tends to obviate any such defense. Even if we agreed to enforce the prevalent morality, we should still have to accommodate the inevitability of change and the propriety of debating and criticizing given practices and values.[14] It is ironic, therefore, that admitting the connection between law and morality generates a conceptual difficulty every bit as strenuous as that facing the positivist theory of law. Moderate theorists, like Hart, who oppose "legal moralism"—the legal enforcement of determinate morality as such and the legal punishment of immorality as such—still favor the view, more or less congruent with Mill's, that the legal coercion of individuals *can* be justified on the grounds of "preventing harm to others" (not, as Mill holds, exclusively on such grounds), though never, by such enforcement, merely to improve or better one's own or another's life.[15] What Hart never satisfactorily resolves is the question, precisely, whether putative harm to others falls *within* the scope of the prevailing morality or is somehow specified independently of such considerations. Unless he resolved it, Hart could be easily recaptured: his opponents hold, perhaps, that particular standards of sexual conduct and decency must be enforced; and Hart himself is driven to hold that, where prevailing standards of harming another are in danger of being violated, with due attention to qualifications precluding mere arbitrariness *and* inconsistency with other moral values, legal enforcement is defensible. Thus, Hart says (reasonably enough), that "the fundamental objection [speaking against legal moralism] surely is that a right to be protected from the distress which is inseparable from the bare knowledge that others are acting in ways you think wrong, cannot be acknowledged by anyone who recognizes individual liberty as a value."[16]

One difficulty confronting Hart's view stems from his conditional admission of substantive rights that might themselves be part of a morality to be legally enforced. A more serious difficulty confronting all moderate theories depends on the ingenuity, however sincere, with which substantive views of what is harmful and not harmful can be made invulnerable to any challenge about interfering with liberty or the like. Hart may have succeeded in demonstrating that, *within a certain moderate liberal tradition*, it is simply not tenable to enforce morality as such—where what is *meant* is that it is untenable to enforce a *certain* determinate set of moral practices. He has not demonstrated and could not demonstrate that it is untenable to enforce *some* portion of morality as such—where, how much and what may be enforced *depends on the moral tradition involved*. Admit homosexuality, bigamy, abortion, prostitution, pornography, suicide, and euthanasia to be intrinsically harmful and one renders their legal enforcement entirely defensible on Hart's own conditions, though not, perhaps, according to Hart's own conscience.[17]

The argument turns us back to Turk's positivistic definition of criminality, relieved of any privileged claims about the relation between "is" and "ought" and about the prospects of scientific jurisprudence.[18] Reconsider that thesis now, in the light of the continuity of criminal law and the disparate values of distinct social aggregates. In this connection, Turk approvingly cites the following thesis of Edwin Sutherland's:

> [Crime] is part of a process of conflict of which law and punishment are other parts. This process begins in the community before the law is enacted, and continues in the community and in the behavior of particular offenders after punishment is inflicted. This process seems to go on somewhat as follows: A certain group of people feel that one of their values—life, property, beauty of landscape, theological doctrine—is endangered by the behavior of others. If the group is politically influential, the value important, and the danger serious, the members of the group secure the enactment of a law and thus win the cooperation of the State in the effort to protect their value. The law is a device of one party in conflict with another party, at least in modern times. Those in the other group do not appreciate so highly this value which the law was designed to protect and do the thing which before was not a crime, but which has been made a crime by the cooperation of the State. This is a continuation of the conflict which the law was designed to eliminate, but the conflict has become larger in one respect, in that the State is now involved. Punishment is another step in the same conflict.[19]

We have already noted the circularity of Turk's definition: criminality is said to be the state of being legally punishable, but punishment is said to be a species of legal penalty appropriate only to crime. Again, although it is true that law and morality develop conjointly, it is not part of the actual law to test for the presence of criminality *by* reference to the ulterior moral values of a community. Certainly, it would be part of the *theory* of criminal law to hold that the violation of substantive moral values, legally encoded, is at least a sufficient condition of criminality; but that condition could also support a theory of extreme relativism, the claim that criminal categories are entirely arbitrary, even the cynicism of Thrasymachus (if better defended than by Thrasymachus himself). Sutherland's thesis, then, is of limited value since it provides no basis for justifying any set of determinate criminal distinctions.

Something more is needed, if institutions as powerful as the criminal law are not to be construed as merely arbitrary, conventional, and coercively favorable to the interests of some politically dominant party. This is not to deny that the criminal law is a coercive instrument. But whatever defense is possible cannot be rendered in terms of historical contingencies alone. There is a way to resolve the issue, but it would not comfort those who subscribe to a fixed law of nature or who adhere to the moderate view that the defense of legal norms rests on an appreciation of the normative political and moral convictions of a society. The issue concerns what has usefully been contrasted as the *legitimacy* and *legality* of statutes. "The authority of law," Carl Friedrich holds,

> rests upon its reasonableness—that is to say, its justice—that the legitimacy of a constitution, a statute, or a decision rests upon its rightfulness, and that its legality rests upon its accord with the positive laws. The same may be said of the "bearers" of authority, legitimacy, and legality, the rulers or sovereigns. Their legality is a question of positive law, particularly of constitutional law, if there is such a law; their legitimacy is a question of right and justice, and their authority a question of reasonableness, that is to say, their ability to realize the ideas, values, the beliefs of the community's members.[20]

But, of course, the "reasonableness" of metalegal criticism seeking legitimacy must be construed either as a search for formal consistency within a given system, or as a rule of fair compromise among recognized elements within a given society, or as a rule for exacting conformity to an undisputed principle of justice within a given society; or else it must be construed as tantamount to a retreat to some form of the natural law doctrine. In short, in this regard, there is no difference in principle between moderates like Hart and Friedrich and natural lawyers, though there is obviously a difference between them in what may be called a matter of legal taste. Within the options provided, a rejection of the natural law thesis appears to drive us either to positivism or to various forms of legal relativism that are themselves, at bottom, forms of positivism *manqué*. In this sense, law, including criminal law, is, as the Marxists have emphasized, another instrument of coercion and exploitation justified only ideologically; although Marxism itself, it must be remembered, claims, in effect, to be a science of normative history. So seen, Marxism is a historicized natural law doctrine.

Definitions of criminality like Turk's are formulated only in terms of legality, not of legitimacy; and attempts to understand the criminal law in terms of a society's ulterior values only strain, through alternative persuasions, toward legitimacy. That even natural law fails to reveal univocal rules and judgments testifies to the absence of an adequate conceptual defense of the details of positive criminal law, in terms of legitimacy.

Step back from the argument, now, and reconsider the larger issues. Criminal law is only a part of positive law; conviction of a crime, and only conviction, entails legal liability to punishment. There is no possibility of defending that institution, unless whoever is held liable can, in principle, be shown to have harmed another or to have harmed society or to have posed the threat of harm in some suitably serious way. But the concept of harming another falls within the minimal concern of any system that could be called a moral system. Hence, criminal law cannot fail to embody at least a portion of favored moral values, particularly those that conform with the dominant interests of powerful parties within society. This is sufficient to insure the constitutional legality of criminal statutes and judgments, but their legitimacy depends, in principle, on the prospect of objectively discerning the relevant moral norms themselves. Under the circumstances, positive criminal law cannot but reflect the partisan values of politically dominant aggregates; and, in the absence of a reasoned defense of a natural law doctrine or of some suitably potent alternative metamoral principle, that is, an overriding principle of conduct,[21] we could not possibly *legitimate* the positive criminal law of any society.

Crime and criminality are distinctions, of course, inherent to any complex society. All that is required is a conception of law and convictions about what constitutes harm to a person or society: to develop an institution for legally enforcing constraints on causing harm is, effectively, to develop the concept of criminality. In this sense, admitting the concept is not in the least tendentious. But, in a diachronic setting, in which the legitimacy of criminal law cannot be objectively confirmed, it is obvious that the confidence with which criminal categories are supported, and the practice of legal punishment, will always be threatened by doubts regarding dominant conceptions of harm. This is especially clear in two subdivisions of the criminal law. One concerns what we usually call political crimes: treason, espionage, sedition, war crimes, disrespect of the state, and the like.[22] The other concerns what have come to be termed, anomalously, "crimes without victims" (or "victimless crimes"): prostitution, gambling, homosexuality, suicide, drug addiction, and the like.[23]

The tendentiousness of what are variously termed political crimes may be shown quite straightforwardly. For one thing, if we admit that the legitimacy of law and political organization must converge in a given society, then what is technically a totalitarian conception of the state, namely, that the state is omnicompetent, insures that there need be no limit to the specification of political crimes or any recourse, in principle, against its judgments. Hitler is said to have held, for instance, that "the total state must not know any difference between law and ethics."[24] The theory of human rights, at bottom, is incompatible with the totalitarian state—in terms of legitimacy, be it noted, *not* in terms of legality; for it is quite possible, on the provision of a suitable ideology, that human rights may be taken to be realized only in serving the state. The thesis that so-called human rights provide a source of political legitimacy independently of the state's power constrains the state and, as in liberal constitutional theory, limits the extension of the concept of political crimes. Consequently, any increase in state power in the direction of totalitarianism conditionally provides a basis for the enlargement of specifically political crimes. A second consideration is this: such political entities as nations and states, as opposed to politically aggregated individuals, are ideologically generated fictions said to have interests, to have various kinds of competence, and to be capable of being harmed.[25] Hence, specifically political crimes, the range of which tends to exhibit the greatest variability and arbitrariness, cannot but reflect the partisan political values of a dominant party. Offenses against the state are offenses against a palpable fiction. The ideology that generates a conviction that the state *has* interests generates as well a receptivity regarding crimes against the state. In our own time, the possibilities may be traced through the Dreyfus affair, the political trials of the Stalinist era, the Nazi abuse of legal formalities, the McCarthy hearings, and the kangaroo courts of the Chinese Cultural Revolution. The concept of political crime is ineliminable, in the sense that the recognition of the state or surrogate entities is pragmatically unavoidable; in fact, the specification of crimes against the state is itself one of the principal means of confirming its "existence" and authority.

At the other end of the spectrum are to be found the so-called victimless crimes. These are all based on a single consideration: the "victim" has harmed himself or made himself accessible to harm and it is criminal so to act. By extension, anyone contributing to such self-harm may be criminally liable as well, for instance, as in homosexual advances. Of course, where relationships among persons are involved, as in prostitution, gambling, and the like, other sorts of criminal offense may obtain. What needs to be noted is the asymmetry between talk of harming others and harming oneself. It is impossible to develop a conception of self-harm without a full-fledged theory of human happiness, normality, natural function or the like, but it is quite possible to develop a conception of harming others without such a theory. The difference goes to the heart of the issue.

Consider, for instance, suicide and murder. A man may act as a fully rational agent in taking his own life. Consequences to others aside, the only way to charge a would-be suicide with a crime requires that his act be construed as intrinsically contrary to that sort of morally admissible conduct that legitimates the criminal law. In England, the Suicide Act (1961) abrogated the law, operative perhaps from the fourteenth or fifteenth century, that attempted suicide was a criminal offense; however, the act "made it a criminal offense to aid, abet, counsel, or procure the suicide of another person."[26] There are parallels respecting other victimless crimes.[27]

The point is that the bearing of one's conduct on another invites considerations of the putative interests of that other that may have been violated or harmed. If we suppose an agent to be rational and to have acted voluntarily, then, leaving aside the care of the weak and defective, which after all is not a *criminal* matter, we can condemn "crimes against oneself" only on the grounds of the violation of some "natural" obligation or the like.[28] On that principle, "victimless crimes" involving relationships between at least two persons and the initiative of someone who is not the "victim" effectively violate the intent of such an obligation. In a word, assuming the prudential concerns of the race *but not any theory of natural law or natural function,* we may construe criminal laws as laws forbidding the violation of the putative prudential interests of others. In this sense, criminal law is a selective institutionalization of prudence that need not be made to rest on dubious doctrines. But crimes against oneself presuppose just such doctrines.

The beauty of the thesis lies in this. The concern of morality, minimally, is the appraisal and control of conduct affecting another. Every moral code, no matter what its partisan persuasion, occupies itself with the management of the prudential concerns of men; every such code is opposed to the *harming* of another. This is not to say that taking another's life is never legally defensible; it is only to say that no such act can fail to be morally significant, can fail to require moral review, and that, for that very reason, the issue is liable to come under the control of the positive criminal law of a particular society.[29] What is true of taking another's life is true of every important prudential concern. Within *that* context, what is criminal is *whatever* is designated as criminal. Anything classified as criminal that is not clearly linked to some moral elaboration of a fundamental prudential concern is obviously arbitrarily so designated (imagine making it a criminal offense merely to look at the tops of trees).

Prudence, at least statistically, is the typical concern of human beings to preserve themselves, their interests, their comfort, their associates, and their enterprises. Whatever threatens such concerns threatens harm. Morality, by means of a favored doctrine, systematizes the "proper" conduct of a society vis-à-vis such concerns. And the criminal law represents a formalization of such prudential objectives as are thought, within a society, to require enforcement by the state or surrogate authority. It is in this sense that crime and criminality are socially ineliminable. No complex society can fail to institutionalize its prudential concerns so as to generate its own criminal law.

Criminal law, then, is distinctly convergent, in the sense that the prudential concerns of the race are based on a realistic appraisal of statistical regularities. There simply are no human societies that are so deviant that they cannot be said to have been concerned, in the aggregate, with the objectives sketched. Nevertheless, no society can be restricted to merely prudential objectives, for they are basically only the facilitating concerns by which ulterior interests are effectively sustained. To admit this is effectively to admit that, within limits, we are captured by the norms and institutions of our own society. We cannot give these up in any simple sense, because we ourselves develop as we do by internalizing just such norms and institutions; and yet, an enlightened review cannot but persuade us of their contingency. Here, rationality requires no more than the piecemeal elimination of observed arbitrariness and incoherence. Substantive changes in the criminal law, as in the whole of law, depend entirely on the determinate forms of our prudential and moral concerns. And these, as far as anyone can tell, remain, beyond the minimal constraints already conceded, entirely subject to the vagaries of contingent history. In that sense, there is, in Lord Devlin's words, a "public morality"—a part of which the criminal law cannot but enforce, on pain of contradiction. But the reason this is so is a matter of logic: it is not because the morals of a society are "those standards of conduct which the reasonable man approves," certainly not because the "reasonable man" would quite naturally approve Christian or utilitarian morals or anything of the kind.[30] It is simply that the concept of harm, which the criminal law articulates, is necessarily linked to the concept of the morally relevant good of a given population.

Notes

1. For a general review and criticism of this sort of optimism, see Barbara Wootton, *Social Science and Social Pathology* (London: Allen & Unwin, 1959); Thomas S. Szasz, *Law, Liberty and Psychiatry* (New York: Macmillan, 1963); Nicholas N. Kittrie, *The Right to be Different* (Baltimore: Johns Hopkins Press, 1971); Seymour L. Halleck, *Psychiatry and the Dilemmas of Crime* (New York: Harper & Row, 1967). The most extreme views, positing biologically determined criminal propensities, appear in such accounts as those of Cesare Lombroso, *Crime, Its Causes and Remedies*, trans. H. P. Horton (Boston: Little Brown, 1911) and Ernest A. Hooton, *Crime and the Man* (Cambridge: Harvard University Press, 1939).

2. For instance, consider the inherent difficulty of such claims as those of H. J. Eysenck viewing criminality as a function of a genetic predisposition to conditionability and position on an introversion-extroversion scale, in *Crime and Personality* (Boston: Houghton Mifflin, 1964).

3. Austin T. Turk, *Criminality and Legal Order* (Chicago: Rand McNally, 1969), p. 25.

4. Ibid., pp. 18, 21-22. Halleck cites W. L. Marshall and W. L. Clark, "The Legal Definition of Crime and Criminals," in *A Treatise on the Law of Crimes* (Chicago: Callaghan, Callaghan, 1952): "Crime can be defined as 'any act or omission prohibited by public law for the protection of the public and made punishable by the state in a judicial proceeding in its own name,' " p. 3.

5. Turk, *Criminality and Legal Order*, pp. 10, 11.

6. See Hans Kelsen, *General Theory of Law and the State* (Cambridge: Harvard University Press, 1945); and Lon L. Fuller, *The Law in Quest of Itself* [Boston: Beacon, 1966 (first published, 1940)].

7. See Fuller, *The Law in Quest of Itself*.

8. Ibid.

9. Norman St. John-Stevas, *Life, Death and the Law* (Bloomington: Indiana University Press, 1961), pp. 29-30.

10. See Carl Joachim Friedrich, *The Philosophy of Law in Historical Perspective*, 2d ed. (Chicago: University of Chicago Press, 1963), Chs. 18-19; also, St. John-Stevas, *Life, Death and the Law*, Ch. 1. See also the earnest effort of Lon L. Fuller to recover the natural law thesis, by analogy with the "natural laws of carpentry," *The Morality of Law* (New Haven: Yale University Press, 1964), especially Ch. 3.

11. St. Thomas Aquinas, *Summa Theologica*, I.-II. Q. XC, art. 4; cited by St. John-Stevas, *Life, Death and the Law*.

12. H. L. A. Hart, *Law, Liberty, and Morality* (Stanford: Stanford University Press, 1963), Lecture I; and St. John-Stevas, *Life, Death and the Law*, p. 35. The statement is from Report of the Committee on Homosexual Offences and Prostitution, London, H. M. S. O. Cmd. 247, September 1957, para. 13.

13. The argument is advanced against the accounts of Lord Devlin, *The Enforcement of Morals* (Oxford: Oxford University Press, 1959) and James Fitzjames Stephen, *Liberty, Equality, Fraternity*, 2d ed. (London: Smith, Elgard, 1874), Preface. Lord Devlin's adjusted argument and other of the most pertinent contemporary statements have been collected in Richard A. Wasserstrom, ed., *Morality and the Law* (Belmont: Wadsworth, 1971).

14. See Richard Wollheim, "Crime, Sin, and Mr. Justice Devlin," *Encounter* 12(1959); 34-40.

15. Hart, *Law, Liberty, and Morality*, Lecture I.

16. Ibid., Lecture II.

17. See H.L.A. Hart, *The Concept of Law* (Oxford: Clarendon, 1961), particularly Ch. 9, which both supports and explicates Hart's moderate position and undermines his general thesis.

18. See Joseph Margolis, *Values and Conduct* (New York: Oxford University Press, 1961), Pt. I.

19. Turk, *Criminality and Legal Order*, pp. xii-xiii.

20. Friedrich, *The Philosophy of Law in Historical Perspective*, Ch. 21. Friedrich attributes the distinction particularly to Carl Schmitt, *Legalität und Legitimität*/(1932) and Guglielmo Ferrero, *Pouvoir* (1942). He also apparently feels that this thesis adequately justifies the dismissal of Kelsen's positivism—which, as he rightly shows, is open to criticism on internal grounds; see Ch. 18.

21. See Margolis, *Values and Conduct*, Pt. II.

22. See Michael Walzer, *Obligations: Essays on Disobedience, War, and Citizenship* (Cambridge: Harvard University Press, 1970).

23. For instance, see Norval Morris, "Crimes Without Victims. The Law is a Busybody," *The New York Times Magazine*, 1 April 1973, pp. 10-11, 58-62.

24. Cited by Hannah Arendt, *The Origins of Totalitarianism*, 2d ed. (New York: World, 1951), Ch. 12; the reference is from Isaac Deutscher, *Stalin: A Political Biography* (London: Oxford University Press, 1949), p. 381.

25. See Ch. 4 of this volume.

26. Erwin Stengel, *Suicide and Attempted Suicide*, 2d ed. (Harmondsworth: Penguin, 1969), pp. 70-72.

27. See St. John-Stevas, *Life, Death and the Law*, Appendices; and Turk, *Criminality and Legal Order*, Ch. 5.

28. See Margolis, *Values and Conduct*, Ch. 8.

29. See Joseph Margolis, "The 'Moral' and the 'Rational,' " *Journal of Value Inquiry* 11(1972): 286-93.

30. Lord Devlin, "Morals and the Criminal Law," in Wasserstrom, *Morality and the Law*. See also Ronald Dworkin, "Lord Devlin and the Enforcement of Morals," reprinted in Wasserstrom, *Morality and the Law*.

6

Punishment

Capital punishment is the most extreme penalty the state can impose on criminal offenders, simply because the successfully executed sentence precludes, like suicide, any further relationships or endeavors of a meaningful sort involving the decedent. The taking of life, however, was not always regarded as the sole prerogative of the state: in early Rome, for instance, fathers apparently had the right to take the lives of their sons for cause, without being held accountable by the state. But in what we are pleased to call advanced societies, capital punishment requires the action of the highest relevant civil authority; and there, its defensibility has long been seriously questioned. The matter is complex because not only is the extremity and irreversibility of execution worrisome, the logic of the very concept of punishment is uncertain. What is it that we do to people when we punish them, and what possible basis could there be for taking another's life *as a form of punishment?*

Capital punishment cannot be a form of chastisement, since chastisement requires that the offender continue to appreciate the point of being punished, after the fact. As far as the offender is concerned, capital punishment serves no corrective or rehabilitative function or even a deterrent function (in the usual sense). Conceivably, it might serve as a deterrent to others or it might be defended as retribution or in other ways; but then, we would be bound to ask for a general accounting of the practice of punishment, in terms of which this particularly radical practice could be understood.

Two further cautions seem useful here: one, that we distinguish between the conceptual defense of the general institution of punishment and the detailed defense, on the basis of preferred values, of particular forms of punishment; second, that we consider the possibility that punishment may not need to be defended, either as a general institution or as a particular set of practical measures, in terms of a single principle or a single set of values. For instance, one might defend capital punishment in retributive terms and the punishment of petty theft in rehabilitative terms; it is not implausible to treat the threat of capital punishment as having a deterrent function, whereas mitigating punishment for petty theft could be justified in rehabilitative, or perhaps retributive, terms rather than in terms of deterrence. In general, it is not clear what all forms of punishment have in common.

If we look at actual penal institutions, the picture is appalling. There is little doubt that current practices in prisons and penitentiaries have no or almost no rehabilitative efficacy or deterrent effect even with regard to the most serious crimes; serve to some extent to improve criminal skills and to confirm criminal tendencies or cynicism about the institution of punishment itself; count very often as a strategy for paralyzing the power and freedom of certain sectors of the community; impose extraordinarily heavy financial costs on a sustaining society almost oblivious of its day-to-day routines or social benefit; degrade, to an enormous extent, the lives of those punished, in terms of sexual relations, violence, loss of family and community contacts, difficulty in engaging in productive work, and the like; and set no example at all of a quality of life those being punished might either imitate or respect or hope to achieve for themselves.[1] Moreover, since men are legally punished on being convicted of a crime, disputes about the justice of the very institutions said to be breached suggest how flimsy the basis may be for a complex practice that metes out, within its competence, such determinate sentences as capital punishment, life imprisonment, imprisonment for ten years at hard labor, thirty days in the workhouse, or suspended sentence.

William Kneale has very conveniently preserved a statement of Barbara Wootten's that seems to anticipate radical changes in the institution of punishment, if not its transformation into something entirely different.[2] "Forget responsibility," he reports her as saying, "and we can ask, not whether an offender ought to be punished, but whether he is likely to benefit from punishment."[3] To speak thus is to combine questions about the concept of punishment and the utility of particular forms of punishment. Certainly, as Kneale and others have made clear, punishment is conceptually related to responsibility; to disallow responsibility as a necessary condition is to preclude anything that could legitimately be called punishment and to permit certain familiar anomalies (the punishment of the innocent, for instance); and to theorize about the benefits of punishment without reference to responsibility leads to absurdity.

For instance, Moritz Schlick once held that "punishment is an educative measure, and as such is a means to the formation of motives, which are in part to prevent the wrongdoers from repeating the act (reformation) and to prevent others from committing a similar act (intimidation)."[4] On this basis, Schlick viewed punishment as "concerned only with the institution of causes, of motives of conduct,"[5] and he went so far as to claim that "the true wrongdoer" was "not identical with . . . the original instigator of the act" ("for the great-grandparents of the man, from whom he inherited his character, might in the end be the cause, or the statesmen who are responsible for his social milieu") and that we assign responsibility *and* punishment where we most reasonably expect to influence the commission of similar acts either by the same agent or others. Since punishment is viewed as future-oriented deterrence (and possibly as a certain form of character formation), and since, in Schlick's view, no one can be regarded as unquestionably innocent, the distribution of punishment must be rationally determined on the basis *only* of the efficiency with which the likelihood of future crimes may be reduced. To put the matter most directly, Schlick confuses normative prescriptions and causal descriptions. He does understand the difference—he insists on it—but he seems to believe that punishing concerns causal efficacy alone, not legal or moral verdicts, possibly because, in some loose sense, we are all more or less equally responsible for whatever crimes are committed.[6] In a word, he confuses punishment and social engineering, whether or not punishment effectively serves the ends to be engineered.

The absurdity of Schlick's thesis and the absurd leanings of Barbara Wootten's show that utilitarian conceptions of punishment can only be provided, if they can be plausibly provided at all, for the grading and ranking of alternative practices under which *those punishable* may be punished, punished in what way and to what advantage. Merely determining who is liable to be punished and on what grounds rests on a formal consideration that cannot be captured by attention to any of the possible consequences of particular punitive practices. In effect, Schlick and Wootten conflate the essential function of punishment with the ulterior functions particular practices of punishment may be made to serve, after liability has been established.

Grant only that every viable society has a system of rules, prescriptive laws, normative institutions, and traditions, and that it is seriously concerned with breaches of such rules. Merely to have violated a prescriptive regulation is to be responsible or accountable for the breach and to be liable for whatever censure, penalty, or punishment is authorized for those found responsible. The concept of punishment, therefore, is distinctly dependent on, and subordinate to, other concepts concerned with obligatory and forbidden behavior. Challenge ulterior institutions regarding what is forbidden or required: inevitably, one calls into question whatever punitive practices they underlie. Challenge, for instance, the legitimacy of the military draft for the Vietnam War and one cannot but challenge the defensibility of punishing those found guilty of avoiding the draft. Nevertheless, no considerations of this sort bear in the least on the eliminability of the institution of punishment itself. If there are prescriptions regarding what is forbidden and obligatory, what is permissible and impermissible, then there must be a form of censure or penalty that a society provides against those duly found to have violated such prescriptions. It does not matter, in *this* respect, how arbitrary or mean or careless the imposed restrictions may be: it is simply a form of inconsistency, an inconsistency between belief and practice,[7] for a society to take behavior seriously enough to regulate it in terms of what is forbidden and obligatory and utterly to ignore or take no formal notice of breaches of those very restrictions. Primitive taboos, Nazi race laws, and the most enlightened legislation imaginable are constrained in precisely the same way in this respect. Still, our thesis about consistency has been put too loosely.

Punishment, as has been suggested, is a formal notion. Relevant regulations are taken as authorized—whether by positive law, moral tradition, revelation, or otherwise does not matter here. Those who break the regulations are accountable: they may, in fact, be blamed for the breach. To be blamed is at least to be censured, which is more than merely to be found accountable: to be accountable justifies the authorization of censure, penalty, or punishment. So if there are prescriptions regarding what is obligatory and forbidden, there must be *some* provision as well both for verdicts or findings of responsibility and for assigning a measure of penalty to whoever is thus found accountable. There are, then, two interlocking linkages relating prescriptions and punishment: one, linking prescriptions and responsibility or accountability; the other, linking accountability and penalty, whether censure, punishment, or something else. The connections between these three are necessary, not in the sense that one entails the other but rather in the sense that our beliefs about prescriptions cannot be consistent with our behavior unless some form of penalty is authorized in the name of the source of the prescriptions and some form of judging accountability is authorized as an intermediary step in justifying the application of sanctions, punishment, or the like. The imposition of penalties is, in effect, a sign of the seriousness with which what is obligatory and forbidden is publicly marked as such.

Consequently, regardless of the differences among them, censure, sanctions, fines, penalties, and punishment all concern imposing some form of deprivation or undesirable pain or undesirable status on those found accountable for relevant breaches. It may, of course, turn out that a given bit of punishment is not *felt* as punishment. For instance, a vagrant thrown in jail may have found a bed for the night. The concept requires only that there be publicly defined conditions of deprivation or undesirable treatment. They must be realistic, in the sense that they must be *generally* so viewed; otherwise, they would not be compatible with the seriousness of the breaches noted. But they need not always be painful or undesirable in the psychological sense.[8] In fact, they could not be counted on to be such unless every would-be penalty or punishment took into account the peculiarities of everyone thus liable. Thrashing, for instance, regularly authorized for a kind of breach, would then not be authorized for persons known to be flagrantly masochistic; and that would deprive punishment of a relevant sort of universality, that need not preclude "second order" adjustment, matching the determinate nature of the offense committed. It would also set conditions that would relate punishment more to the contingent nature of the particular persons affected, characteristically irrelevant to the offenses committed, than to the particular nature of the offenses themselves. Censure, penalty, and punishment, then, are formulated with an eye to general psychological tendencies, in virtue of which they may be expected to be taken as such; but, on pain of arbitrariness and even injustice, they cannot be adjusted in terms of severity merely to accommodate the idiosyncratic mental states of those affected.

It is possible that leniency and severity be relevantly considered but only in terms of secondary prescriptions that obtain once liability is established, applying, say, to first offenders, repeated offenders, clear and present danger, the interests of others affected, and the like. Here, then, is clarified one defensible sense in which "the punishment fits the crime": it fits the crime, not whoever happens to be the criminal. In that sense, the fit is purely formal, has nothing whatsoever to do with the propriety of particular forms of punishment, concerns only the relevance of punishment itself, and provides a necessary condition for any hardship's being a case of punishment.

These considerations undermine the famous quarrel about the justification of punishment, between so-called utilitarians and retributivists. "It is not," as A.M. Quinton points out, "that we *may* not punish the innocent and *ought* only to punish the guilty, but that we can*not* punish the innocent and *must* only punish the guilty."[9] The charge, of course, must be put in terms of belief, since errors in justice are not impossible. But utilitarianism is not needed to justify the institution of punishment: that depends on the implications merely of defining crimes and offenses in the context of human behavior; at best, the utilitarian can be expected to offer a defense of particular forms of punishment as, in accord with his ulterior principle, appropriately embodying the institution granted. And the retributivist is either a utilitarian who holds that an offender's paying the "fitting" penalty is intrinsically good for all, regardless of ulterior consequences; or else he holds that it is mere justice that he pay thus or that it is a matter of mere revenge; otherwise, he means to defend retribution in the vacuous, but quarrelsome, sense that whoever is punished is judged punishable—which returns us to the question of the meaning of "punishment" and leaves entirely open the defense of particular practices. We can ask for a defense of punishment, in an interesting sense, only in terms of why we should punish *in this way or that.* The bare institution calls for defense only because people may not realize that the seriousness they assign to crimes and offenses rationally commits them to holding offenders liable to penalty, punishment or the like.

Not enough has been said to distinguish punishment from penalty, censure, or forfeiture. In recent years, the point has been missed by nearly all who have sought to specify the defining marks of punishment, usually construed as pain or some undesirable status inflicted on someone, for alleged offenses or infractions, by a suitable authority.[10]

It is possible that one may punish *by* censure, penalty, or fine; but it does not follow that every instance of censure, penalty, or fine is an instance of punishment. Much hangs on this. A football team may be penalized when one of its players is offsides, but the team need not be punished; still, the team's manager may punish a player for being repeatedly careless, possibly by fining him. One pays a traffic ticket as a fine but not, normally, as a punishment; and yet, repeated traffic violations may lead to conviction and punishment for flouting the law.

There is, however, a surprisingly straightforward distinction to be made out between penalty and punishment, taken as alternative forms of treating offenders. *Penalties* may be assigned to persons *qua* functionaries, officeholders, occupying special relationships, roles, or parts; but *punishment* is invariably assigned to persons *qua* persons. A man is punished because he has murdered or been guilty of theft; but, characteristically, a motorist is fined and a football team penalized. Similarly, we censure the governor for failing to endorse this or that legislation, but we imprison the man for malfeasance while in office. Men are responsible for what they do *qua* men and *qua* functionaries. But it is as persons and not as functionaries that we are said to cause *harm to another.* Punishment, but not penalty or fine, presupposes guilt with respect to positive harm.

Obviously, the distinction corresponds to prevailing doctrines about the seriousness of the behavior of men *and* about the proper characterization of the agents involved. After all, soldiers, engineers, physicians, fathers, neighbors, friends, dogcatchers, postmen, wives, priests, and bystanders are always, also, men and women; and the behavior of men and women may always be viewed in this or that restricted respect. To punish a man is to hold *him* accountable for some harm; to dock a waitress for breaking dishes is to penalize the waitress, the woman *qua* waitress, in accord with some implied contract, no matter how minor. This is why no stigma attaches to penalties unless one begins to hold the full person responsible. Parking violators pay their fines by mail more in the spirit of paying a fee that in the spirit of suffering punishment. The very anonymity is instructive, because one cannot be punished unless he is suitably addressed or confronted as a person.

The distinction between punishment and penalty has been notably considered by Joel Feinberg.[11] Feinberg holds:

> punishment is a conventional device for the expression of attitudes of resentment and indignation, and of judgments of disapproval and reprobation, on the part either of the punishing authority himself or of those "in whose name" the punishment is inflicted. Punishment,

in short, has a *symbolic significance* largely missing from other kinds of
penalties. [12]

From this point of view, punishment is itself the expression of the
community's condemnation, disapproval, or disavowal; that is, the
expressive function is said to be just what is essential to anything's
being an instance of punishment. The thesis conveniently explodes all
speculation about merely matching the severity of offense and pain or
deprivation, revenge or retribution in that sense, and shows the altogether subordinate character of speculating about the form particular
punishment ought to take (utilitarian considerations, for instance,
deterrence or rehabilitation). But, although it nicely distinguishes between penalty and punishment, since whoever is merely penalized is
not thereby condemned for what he has done, or even disapproved of
or disavowed, it does not distinguish satisfactorily between, say, censure and punishment or even explain why those penalized are not also
punished. Feinberg's account shows convincingly why it is a matter of
definition that punishment impose hard treatment on an offender, not
hard treatment rather than soft, but hard treatment as the non-verbal
or verbal expression of resentment, indignation, disapproval, or reprobation. On occasion, penalties that are not forms of punishment,
tax-return fines, for instance, may be more severe than those meted
out as forms of punishment. The difference must lie in what is sym-
bolized: in penalties, the symbolic function may be all but lost; in
punishment, it is essential.

We have, in effect, observed at least two qualifications of the expressive theory of punishment: one, that punishment is always assigned to
the whole person, for causing or posing a threat of positive harm, and
that penalties are assigned to persons as functionaries or in particular,
often highly specialized or institutionalized, roles, where no harm
need be presupposed; the other, that punishment is meted out to
persons by addressing or confronting them in some suitable ceremonial way and that penalties do not require a form of address. The
penalty imposed on a football team for being offsides is not only a
hardship imposed but also, perhaps, a symbolic expression of the
umpire's *notice*, but not condemnation, of the team's having failed to
play within the limits of correct as opposed to merely eligible play.
Penalties may have a symbolic function as well, though if they do, they
are likely to concern persons in given roles only; or, *if* they may be said
to concern the whole person, they will characteristically not involve
address, symbolic function (say, when a man must pay a parking fine,
in terms of strict liability), [13] or ascriptions of having caused harm.

Censure is particularly interesting, because condemnation or disapproval *is* involved; characteristically, also, a form of address and a symbolic expression of disapproval, though not necessarily an assumption or a threat of positive harm. Hissing actors at the theater or condemning the president's action in a public letter are forms of censure but not of punishment. One may be tempted to make something of the issue of whether the disapproval or condemnation is authorized or not, but it is conceivable that the Congress merely censure the president for an action within its proper purview, without penalizing or punishing the president in any other respect and, of course, without precluding the possibility of punishing *by* censure.

Minimally, censure is an expression of blame, disapproval, reprobation that issues, formally or informally, from those that have the relevant authority or the relevant right—the people, for instance—in a distinctly public or ceremonial form of address. It may exhibit all the properties thought to be essential to punishment, without actually being punishment. It falls short of punishment, in one way, if it is addressed only to persons *qua* functionaries or officeholders or occupants of specialized roles or relationships. A candidate for public office may censure citizens for their political apathy, for instance. It fails, in another way, if it is not formally construed *as a hardship authorized* because of the relevant breach: in fact, it cannot be a hardship of the relevant sort if it is addressed to persons only in their special roles, though it may entail holding a man responsible for what he has done *qua* functionary.

Censure becomes punishment, however mild it may be, when it is an authorized hardship addressed to the whole person, convicted of having caused harm to others or to the society, whether formally or informally authorized, whether legally or morally. Censure is punishment only when it is a consequence authorized for a duly determined breach of what is required or forbidden: imagine someone censured before his god for a breach of a sacred rule. It is quite possible, as Feinberg supposes, that punishing is an expression (and the only expression) *of* disapproval or condemnation.[14] Nevertheless, the pattern involves an ellipsis; for only if the hardship imposed is authorized in terms of a breach of what is required or forbidden can we speak of punishment. There are, inevitably, two critical "moments" in the pattern of punishment, even if they are conflated: the finding of guilt, accountability, responsibility; and the imposition of a penalty as a hardship justified by that antecedent finding. But if this is so, then punishment is not, unless *per accidens*, simply the expression of disapproval or condemnation; it is what, in terms of consistency between belief and behavior in the context of suitable rules, is warranted by the verdict itself. "Blame," we may say, is a term that signifies not merely assigning responsibility to someone but, also, actually censuring someone already judged responsible, whether such censure counts as punishment or not and whether or not the one blamed can be said to have caused some positive harm (one may, of course, blame or censure a boxer for having lost a fight, where no punishable harm or moral or legal considerations are involved). Censure, then, is not punishment insofar as it is an expression of the justificatory finding plus reprobation; it is punishment only if it is a consequence authorized and imposed in virtue of that finding and the finding concerns a certain serious positive or potential harm.

The quibble is important. There could not be a concept of crime if there were not also a concept of punishment; for crimes are committed only by persons, as breaches of what is forbidden and required, causing or threatening to cause positive harm to others or to society at large. Penalties are hardships, relatively speaking, imposed for cause, but not necessarily for harm; that is why they sometimes involve no form of address at all, except perhaps mere notification. A society that does not authorize punishment for the crimes it identifies (even if, in particular cases, it chooses to waive punishment) can only be supposed to behave inconsistently, to fail to have a coherent grasp of the nature of crime itself. Hence, there can be, and need be, no defense of the bare institution of punishment other than that of an appreciation of the very features of the concept. But to say this is to admit as well that it is entirely reasonable to expect the details of actual systems of punishment to be justified in at least comparative terms.

The critical distinctions are these. Crimes and moral offenses are breaches of rules stipulating what is required and forbidden, whether promulgated by legal or formal public authority or recognized within a tradition. Men are sometimes actually judged accountable for such breaches and held liable for penalty or punishment.[15] They may be *penalized* without being condemned or censured or punished, if the hardship or pain or deprivation authorized be assigned them not as whole persons but merely as persons in this or that role or function or relationship; and though they have broken certain rules, they will not have been judged to have caused or to have threatened to cause harm thereby. They may also be *censured* without being either penalized or punished, if the finding of accountability is merely conflated with an expression of condemnation, disapproval, or reprobation: hence, without imposing any consequential hardship (though, if censure is a hardship, we may view it also as penalty or punishment). And they may be said to be *punished* only if the authorized hardship is imposed as a consequence of having been found accountable, as a person, for the breach alleged, resulting in positive harm or posing a suitable threat.

Two further distinctions are instructive. The first is that, from a formal point of view, punishment or penalty is an expression of the measure of seriousness assigned a given breach of what is forbidden and required. Punishment is not an expression of condemnation but a symbol of the seriousness of the offense condemned, deployed as an authorized consequence.[16] Vengeance or revenge, therefore, is precluded, simply because punishment is not to be understood in terms of psychological dispositions but in terms of formal justice. As it happens, the term "retribution" is used equivocally in these two senses.[17] In terms of justice, then, we may acknowledge a second sense of the expression "the punishment fits the crime": it fits the crime by providing a symbolic measure of the seriousness of the breach. But the question of a proper fit arises only on the retributivist view, on the view that a recognized breach of given rules entails the punishability of the agent: punishment, then, must be a symbolic, *retributive* expression of the graded seriousness of some breach of what is required or forbidden, causing or threatening to cause positive harm; it does not and cannot restore the *status quo ante* or, in *that* sense (the sense proper to revenge), benefit or be useful to anyone (though it may confer benefits).

Having said this, we see at once that all theories of the deterrent and rehabilitative functions of punishment are entirely secondary, concerned with the possible *further* benefits to some institution affected, in a practical sense, by institutionalizing crime and offense. Undoubtedly, there *is* a measure of utility in punishment and the fear of punishment, though all known theories are open to paradoxical applications in practice.[18] Ideally, its utility should correspond to the endorsement, by potential offenders, of a schedule of punishments. In practice, however, whatever utility there is is largely assignable to the perceived effects of what contingently happens to serve as punishment. So utilitarian or consequentialist theories of punishment, including rehabilitative theories, tend not to be focused on the institution as such, as Barbara Wootten's and Moritz Schlick's remarks have already hinted.

No one need draw the conclusion, however, that the reform of punitive practices cannot be undertaken either in terms of justice or in terms of utility. The current dispute about the death penalty is instructive here. As far as can be judged, "there is no evidence from the

statistics that the death penalty is a superior deterrent to imprisonment" (as opposed to the stronger claim that "there is evidence that the
death penalty is not a superior deterrent to imprisonment").[19]

The argument against the death penalty takes two distinct forms. In
one, it may be said that justice precludes that particular penalty; that
whatever appropriate "fit" there may be between serious punishment
and serious crime, execution exceeds propriety. This is perhaps close
to the sense in which the death sentence was set aside by the United
States Supreme Court as "cruel and unusual" punishment. In the
other, it may be said, in the absence of factual evidence to the contrary,
that the ulterior deterrent function of punishment is effectively promoted by penalties short of capital punishment or as effectively promoted as it would be with the addition of capital punishment. This is
perhaps close to the sense in which the *Report of the Royal Commission
on Capital Punishment* (1953) questions the practice.[20]

To put the alternative before us suggests at once how, under the
circumstances, it cannot but be a partisan or tendentious argument to
support or eliminate capital punishment. Whether demanding death
or a less severe penalty "fits" the usual cases of premeditated murder,
airplane hijacking, peddling narcotics, or killing policemen and
prison guards, depends on the strength of competing doctrinal convictions about the "seriousness" of offenses and a fair "fit." The argument that execution is "cruel and unusual" is convincing to some
extent, in view of the prospect that actually carrying the execution out
may be delayed for years; but that, after all, may argue a need to end
the delay. Similarly, objections are compelling to the extent that they
rest on evidence that, say, the sentence is prejudicially applied against
blacks; but, again, the argument fails to engage the issue directly,
which is not to deny that *if* such abuses cannot be corrected, then there
may be overriding reasons for abolishing capital punishment because
there are overriding reasons for reforming the entire criminal justice
system. There is simply no non-partisan way in which to determine
the symbolic appropriateness of capital punishment for those most
serious crimes of premeditated murder for which, historically, it has
been assigned. But *if* this is so, then the very ease with which the death
penalty may be *symbolically replaced* shows the arbitrariness of insisting
that *only* the death penalty will do. The counterpart argument in terms
of utility is obviously simpler, because, on the evidence, it cannot be
shown that the death penalty *is* a stronger deterrent than imprisonment. So, the symbolic function of punishment counts against the
death penalty because death is irreversible, the most extreme penalty
possible, and because whatever symbolism is required can, in princi

ple, be provided in a less extreme sentence. The deterrent function of punishment, not to mention the rehabilitative, counts against the death penalty, because the facts are what they are, or are, on the evidence, what they are taken to be. One may imagine that there are stronger, possibly conclusive, arguments that may be added, but the familiar ones are all tendentious.

The institution of punishment, therefore, marks the enormous seriousness with which society interferes in the lives of individual men, imposing on them conventionally approved sentences for having committed conventionally defined offenses. Here, our partisan energies are drawn in two directions: in disputes about the definition of offenses deserving punishment and in disputes about the specification of penalties fitting given offenses. Beyond these, debate inevitably concerns the use of non-punitive instruments of change and control, against the background of which punishment seems occupied with a kind of civil pathology. Given the relevant definitions, expiation through punishment is, perhaps, psychologically useful and punishment itself, conceptually required. But the mind constantly turns to the underlying evils of a society that produces the very conditions called "crime," that it then turns to prosecute with a professional conscience.

A final consideration. If we think of crime and punishment in terms of the prudential interests of a society,[21] then we cannot help appreciating the relativization of the practice of punishment. Consequently, the criticism of punishment pursues both the ulterior categories of crime (altering which, we alter our liability to punishment) and the extended uses of punishment (reviewing which, we review the proper fit between crime and punishment). To speak of the reform of our prisons is a relatively conservative move. We are embarrassed by an enormous population essentially thwarted, by reason of imprisonment, from pursuing their own interests and essentially "unreconstructed" in terms of the avowed interests of the imprisoning society.[22] But to challenge the categories of crime itself is to intend to alter or reform the underlying ideology of a society. Apart from the persuasiveness of the maneuver, we are forced to attend to the contingency of our punitive practices, particularly the most severe, and to the conceptual difficulty of confirming *any* set of criminal categories that clearly favors, as it must, the interests of one sub-population over those of another. There is no way to escape such reflections and there is no way to eliminate the categories of crime and punishment. But, if so, then we are forced to concede the oddity of pursuing the ulterior uses of punishment, in terms of rehabilitative or deterrent or similar utilitarian goals in the absence of any clear conception of the relative justice of those prevailing social arrangements that crime presumably threatens. It is as easy to argue that a deeper injustice produces most crime as it is to fix a fair punishment for those found guilty. In the nature of the case, the categories of crime and punishment become less plausible as their instances multiply. And, although *some* constraints of fairness are nontendentious, no complex system of law can be completely validated or validated in its essential rules in terms of any known procedure that does not itself favor, on doctrinal grounds, the system in question. Accordingly, the very dependence of the concept of punishment on that of crime, in spite of the circularity endorsed by Turk, argues that wherever the law is relatively severe and adversely affects a substantial, well-demarcated sub-population, the thesis on which the legitimacy of the law actually rests ought to accommodate the conceptions of justice of that population as well.

Notes

1. See *Attica: The Official Report of the New York State Commission on Attica* (New York: Bantam Books, 1972), for the most sustained contemporary study of an American prison; *Struggle for Justice: A Report on Crime and Punishment in America Prepared for the American Friends Service Committee* (New York: Hill and Wang, 1971); and David Rudofsky, *The Rights of Prisoners* (New York: Avon Books, 1973). See also Karl Menninger, *The Crime of Punishment* (New York: Viking, 1968).

2. William Kneale, "The Responsibility of Criminals," Marrett Memorial Lecture, 1967 (Oxford: Clarendon, 1967).

3. Ibid. See also Barbara Wootten, *Social Science and Social Pathology* (New York: Macmillan, 1959).

4. Moritz Schlick, *Problems of Ethics*, trans. David Rynin (New York: Prentice-Hall, 1939), Ch. 7. Compare Jeremy Bentham, *Introduction to the Principles of Morals and Legislation*, Ch. XIII, sec. i.

5. Ibid.; italics added.

6. See, for further discussion, C.A. Campbell, "Is 'Free Will' a Pseudo-problem?" *Mind* 60(1951): 686-706.

7. Cf. further, Joseph Margolis, *Values and Conduct* (New York: Oxford University Press, 1971), Ch. 4.

8. Cf. J. R. Lucas, "Or Else," *Proceedings of the Aristotelian Society* 69(1968-69); reprinted in *Moral Problems*, ed. James Rachels (New York: Harper and Row, 1971).

9. A. M. Quinton, "On Punishment," in *Philosophy, Politics, and Society*, ed. P. Laslett (Oxford: Blackwell, 1956). See also A. Flew, "The Justification of Punishment," *Philosophy* 29(1954): 291-307; and S. I. Benn and R. S. Peters, *Social Principles and the Democratic State* (London: Allen and Unwin, 1959), Ch. 8.

10. Cf. Flew, "The Justification of Punishment."

11. Joel Feinberg, *Doing and Deserving* (Princeton: Princeton University Press, 1970), particularly Ch. 5.

12. Ibid., p. 98.

13. See Richard A. Wasserstrom, "Strict Liability in the Criminal Law," *Stanford Law Review* 12(1960): 731-45.

14. Feinberg, *Doing and Deserving*.

15. The complexities of the concepts of responsibility and liability are systematically explored in another context in Kurt Baier, "Guilt and Responsibility," in *Individual and Collective Responsibility*, ed. Peter A. French (Cambridge: Schenkman, 1972). See also Kurt Baier, "Responsibility and Action," in *The Nature of Human Action*, ed. Myles Brand (New York: Scott Foresman, 1970).

16. Cf. Feinberg, *Doing and Deserving*.

17. Cf. *Report of the Royal Commission on Capital Punishment*, cited in Feinberg, *Doing and Deserving*, p. 101.

18. See for instance Gertrude Ezorsky, "The Ethics of Punishment," in *Philosophical Perspectives on Punishment*, ed. Gertrude Ezorsky (Albany: State University of New York Press, 1972). This is probably the most complete anthology on punishment available. See also Ted Honderich, *Punishment: The Supposed Justifications* (London: Hutchinson, 1969); and Edmund Pincoffs, *The Rationale of Legal Punishment* (New York: Humanities Press, 1966). On the practical side, see Ramsey Clark, *Crime in America* (New York: Simon and Schuster, 1970); and Marvin E. Frankel, *Criminal Sentences* (New York: Hill and Wang, 1972).

19. H. L. A. Hart, "Murder and the Principles of Punishment: England and the United States," *Northwestern University Law Review* 52(1958): 433-61. Hart shows convincingly how difficult it is to appraise the effects of the death *sentence* as opposed to the imminence of *death*, despite the obviously prudentially (one might say, vacuously) convincing argument that the threat of death is, as such, more of a deterrent than the threat of punishment.

20. See Hart, "Murder and the Principles of Punishment"; see also Hugo Bedau, ed., *The Death Penalty in America* (Garden City: Doubleday, 1964).

21. See Chapter 5 of this volume.

22. For a fascinating account of a radically different conception of prisons, see Bao Ruo-wang and Rudolph Chelminski, *Prisoner of Mao* (New York: Coward, McCann and Geoghegan, 1973), where, whatever one may say of the cost, the Chinese prison system must be seen to have a realistically and explicitly ideological rehabilitative function. One cannot, of course, avoid reflecting on the import of Alexander Solzhenitsyn's exposé of the Soviet penal system, in *Gulag Archipelago 1918-1956*, trans. Thomas P. Whitney (New York: Harper and Row, 1973).

7

Illness

Dying is not a disease, though if men tended to be immortal it would be. Illness need not be fatal though it may be, and the regular and ultimately irreversible decline and loss of life are presupposed in every theory of health. For a race radically committed to physical comfort and beauty, pregnancy might very easily be viewed as an infection; and for a society technologically so advanced that what we regard as normal aging could be easily avoided for an interval four times as long as a normal lifespan, "normal aging" might be treated as a sign of disease. Medicine is by no means omnipotent, but to classify bodily states and processes as forms of illness strongly suggests that cures may, in principle, be found. Physicians are thought to be the bearers of that science that detects and characterizes bodily disorders and of that art that restores the body to its appropriate state of health.

But if we ask ourselves what we mean by health and illness and whether and in what way they are fixed once and for all for human beings, we cannot fail to be puzzled. Is hunger an illness? Apparently

not, since the deficiency is ubiquitous, short-termed, regularly satisfied by the intake of food—normally, not under medical prescription.
Is diabetes or vitamin deficiency an illness? Apparently, since it is so
designated, affects the race in an extremely varied way, and requires a
great deal of specialized information about the physiological processes
of the body. Are birthmarks a medically significant defect? Apparently
not, if they are benign and relatively static, even though their causes
and their removal depend on comparably specialized information and
skill. Is obesity a disorder? Yes and no, for it entails particular risks
linked to other admitted disorders and yet fat people may, with proper
care—as much care as others may take with their own diet and
regimen—live as long and as lively a life as anyone else.

The issue is complicated by the concepts of mental illness and
psychosomatic illness. Mental illness, in fact, is a much-debated concept, sometimes said to be incoherent or to depend on an illicit extension of the concept of illness proper to physical medicine.[1] Also,
medicine is a curious discipline in some respects, because it is very
nearly the sole professional specialty that claims the credentials of a
science and renders its judgment chiefly in terms of prescriptive
norms. It does not confine itself, of course, to descriptive and causal
matters but provides diagnoses of defects, deficiencies, abnormalities,
infections, malfunctionings, diseases, illnesses, and disorders—in a
word, various departures from allegedly normal and not merely statistically prevalent modes of human functioning. In so doing, it claims to
identify the norms of health and illness by an application of its own
scientific competence. Nevertheless, particularly where the question
of mental illness arises, the medical catalogue seems, at times, quite
tendentious. Consider that in the psychiatric literature, with much
misgiving and considerable intradisciplinary quarreling, such syndromes as suicide, homosexuality, psychopathy, alcoholism, addiction, and even crime have at one time or another been labeled as
illnesses—not merely noted as capable of being caused by an illness or
of being manifested in a pathological form.[2]

Illness, like life and death, befalls the whole man; although like the
respiratory diseases of miners, it may result from the specialized functions men fulfill. But then, if impotence were construed as an illness
—and why should it or why should it not?—a seemingly specialized
function would be at least implicitly assigned to the whole creature.
The tendency is notable particularly where alleged disorders of a
sexual and social nature are involved, homosexuality and psychopathy
for instance. Here, one's moral persuasion tends to masquerade as
medicine.[3] Ferenczi, for example, actually viewed capitalism as a form

of anal fixation. But the issue is much more subtle, for even where pathological syndromes are not made to depend on some specialized function thought appropriate to human nature or on some partisan moral conviction, the specification of illness cannot escape at least an implied reference to the technological, environmental, and cultural concerns of portions of the race.

Mortality sets limits to medicine and so, to health and illness. Where, in principle, or by an extension of human technology, there is no prospect of adjusting our biological processes, there is no point in speaking of illness or disease. Aging, therefore, is not a disease any more than dying is: we could not begin to consider reclassifying it unless and until we could, within realistic limits, expect to arrest and control its metabolism. The upshot is that even such categories are subject to revision in the light of changing capabilities and changing aspirations. Even the general functions of man are specified in a way that reflects the historical orientation of dominant, conceivably idiosyncratic, populations. A cheap and plentiful chemical detergent that would arrest the accumulation of cholesterol and other bodily sludges and quadruple the life expectancy of a people who deliberately manufacture it and make it available, and who thereupon organize their entire society along lines presupposing a new "normal" life expectancy, would quite naturally revolutionize prevailing conceptions of health and disease. But would it be convincing to hold that other peoples, perhaps remote, lacking their technology, conceivably not even interested in their objectives, could, in terms of such criteria, be objectively said to be in good health or ill? Not that the new measures could not be objectively applied; only that we might wonder whether subscribing to them was a foregone conclusion, the automatic consequence of a "discovery" of science. Still, we do admit discovering new diseases, in the sense of detecting disorders not previously noticed as well as disorders that are the novel result of technologically changed ways of living. And we are prepared, of course, to insist that some disorders are genuine enough, whether or not they are so construed by the society afflicted; otherwise, on the argument, a society radically ignorant of medicine could never be said to suffer any illness at all.

There are limits to relativizing the concepts of health and illness, but those are generous enough to permit us to ascribe a certain understandable bias to medical norms. Since medicine professes, minimally, to treat bodily disorders, we may fairly ask for the least disputable grounds on which the norms of physical health may be specified. And since, by arguable extensions, illness is made to include mental illnesses, behavioral disorders, psychosomatic ailments, even social pathologies (delinquency, crime, violence, addiction), we may ask as well for the least disputable grounds on which the extended norms may be defended. This is not to say that medical judgments are invariably normative: it is quite possible, for instance, to construe the question of increasing one's stamina or eliminating freckling or offsetting the effect of nausea in drinking whole milk as medically pertinent; even so, it is not possible to view all medical judgments as normatively neutral and, in the cases mentioned, a competent judgment must be compatible with relevant normative judgments. In a word, medicine cannot be viewed so that its values are purely hypothetical, as if they depended entirely on the ad hoc objectives of each and every client. No, medicine is an institutionalized specialty devoted to the treatment of illness and the maintenance of health; and these objectives, however arguable or variable, are fixed in some sense for human beings as such.

The essential clue is a simple one. If a person's arm is paralyzed so that it cannot be used for any or nearly all or the preponderant share of whatever projects human beings ordinarily pursue, then paralysis is a significant ailment and we presume that medicine ought to be able to cure it. Such incapacities provide us with evidence of disorder. But the norms of health and illness must be formulated in terms of the least tendentious objectives: this is what is meant in saying that medical norms concern the health of the body, without regard to any culturally determinate interests, or, more controversially, the health of the mind or the health of the person. Still, it is an ellipsis for what we extrapolate from any and all determinate interests in order to preserve the neutrality of the medical arts.

Briefly stated, medicine is a professionalized specialty concerned with a limited range of general *prudential* objectives: just those that depend, minimally, on the state of the body adjusted to enable, so far forth, the realization of such objectives or, by extension, the analogous state of the mind or of the person. Like law, medicine is a prudential art. But where the law is concerned with order among individuals and aggregates, medicine is concerned with the capacity to use our bodies and our minds and ourselves as effective instruments, insofar as all our projects depend on personal exertion of some sort. Nothing that we do can fail to depend on the state of our bodies; consequently, medicine is least likely to be charged with tendentiousness where the requisite norms concern physical health, though, even there, as with evolutionary ethics[4] and arguments regarding eugenic breeding and the like, medicine may incorporate our partisan preferences. Illness, disease, disorder, and malfunction are, in every case, forms of prudentially significant incapacity in which the creature is victimized by a state of its own body or mind. Within the acknowledged limits of mortality, technology, and culturally directed concerns, we require medicine to correct such forms of victimization or at least to explore the means for doing so. Clearly, to define medicine this way is to provide as well a basis for variable conceptions of medical norms. Change the technology of a society, change its environment, change its dominant interests: its medical norms as well as its legal norms will change.

Physical medicine, however, is notably conservative. This is not to deny enormous technical progress in the detection, characterization, and treatment of diseases; it is only to say that inasmuch as the human body has changed comparatively little through the known history of medicine, the detailed application of our prudential norms to the body's various systems has changed comparatively little as well.[5] The most obvious evidence of this lies with our theories of the functions of the various organs of the body. The eye, the heart, and the liver, for instance, are assigned their respective functions with considerable precision and assurance. But what does our doing so mean? It is clear that sight depends on the eye; but to say that sight is the *function* of the eye is to say, also, that the eye is defective insofar as a certain power of sight cannot be sustained by the eye itself.

Here, then, the prudential interests of man, given the range of life that human societies pursue, are served within a certain margin of variation by eyes capable of functioning in certain assignable ways. The prudential norms are *not* assigned by the science of medicine; they represent rather a statistically dominant pattern of determinate interests, as nearly transcultural as possible, that serve the greatest or at least a very great variety of ulterior and overriding objectives. The concept of the health of the eye is as little influenced by partisan values as any normative concept could possibly be: it concerns nothing but the conditions for effective sight for the members of a population in which not a great variation in the range of such effectiveness obtains distributively and in which effectiveness itself is gauged in terms of a standard range of general problems to be solved. On the other hand, should the earth's pollution drive all human societies into the depths of the sea, at a level at which sunlight could not penetrate and artificial light would be impractical to sustain (supposing such an environment capable of supporting human life), there would no longer be a point to insisting that sight was the eye's function.

It may seem a little strained, but we do in fact anthropomorphize the eye, the heart, and the liver in the same way we do the sun (which "functions" to provide the earth's energy), coal (which "functions" as a source of heat and power), eggs (which "function" as a source of protein), and so on. Also, inevitably, we favor the interests of selected contemporary societies. Everything that is significantly useful to man acquires a congruent function—under the authority of our presumptive prudential interests. There is no sense in which the functions of these things are simply discovered by an exercise of science. But then, there is actually no need to discover them; they answer to the detailed ways in which the body's capacities, maintained at a certain level, enable our prudential interests to be served and, instrumentally, the widest possible or a "sufficiently" wide range of ulterior interests as well. Admit such values as preserving life, minimizing pain, maintaining physical strength, and the like: medicine thereupon assigns a certain measure of health to the enabling systems of the body and, by extension, the mind.

In this sense, medical norms are relatively nontendentious; but in this sense, also, medicine is an instrumental discipline whose norms are set by antecedent interests. Prudential norms are natural, in a purely statistical sense; they are not natural if to say they are implies that acting contrary to prudence is inherently irrational or contrary to human nature. As long as prudential objectives are rather naively and casually assigned, in the sense in which they have hardly changed over millenia, medical norms of health and illness preserve their approximate neutrality. But introduce, however plausibly, problems of scarcity, waste, pollution, and overpopulation and the norms become more quarrelsome and professional judgment begins to consider eugenic breeding, the right of the aged and the infirm to die, and the right to discontinue medical assistance. Medicine thereupon intrudes into more and more areas of public policy and even the line between medical authority and police power begins to fade.[6]

It is easy to see the ideological convenience of construing the criminal, the delinquent, the sexual and social deviant, the retarded, the poor, the maladjusted, the insane, the neurotic, the alcoholic, the addict, the malcontent, the revolutionary, and the reactionary as clinical specimens. On the assumption that the norms of health and disease are the discovery of an independent medical science, moral and political forces favoring this or that policy need hardly rely on the persuasiveness of their own doctrines; they need argue only that they are applying the neutral dictates of the science of medicine. Medicine is thus subverted by morality and politics, and they in turn appear to wither away in the name of medicine.[7]

But mental illness needs to be looked at more closely. Consider, for instance, Freud's original challenge to the then-existing medical framework within which he had expected to remain. Freud isolated an

array of physical and behavioral patterns strikingly similar to syndromes already admitted as illnesses by physical medicine but which
appeared to lack an etiology in which such causes as infection, brain
damage, or chemical imbalance could be specified. His speculations
led him to suggest psychogenic and sociogenic causes that he hoped
would reduce to physical factors; furthermore, he explored the possibility of correcting these patterns by a variety of novel techniques,
including narcotics, hypnosis, and verbal exchanges of a certain sort.
The resemblance to standard illnesses, as in hysterical paralysis, was
so marked that he searched first for the usual physical causes; failing,
he turned to other explanations. For these reasons, he *extended* the
term "illness" to the newly isolated syndromes, without a clear sense of
a distinction between deciding questions of fact (were his clients really
ill?) and deciding questions of how to classify the facts (should those
syndromes be termed illnesses?). Were Freud challenged to justify the
extension, granting the strong resemblance between the new cases
and the old, he might have said something about medicine's purpose
of ministering to the disabled.

It is often thought by critics of psychiatry that there is something
conceptually illicit in extending the concept of illness to complexes in
which no infection, no organic dysfunction, or the like is present.
Thomas Szasz, for instance, says:

> I maintain that Freud did not "discover" that hysteria was a mental
> illness. Rather, he advocated that so-called hysterics be declared "ill."
> The adjectives "mental," "emotional," and "neurotic" are simply
> devices to codify—and at the same time obscure—the differences
> between two classes of disabilities or "problems" in meeting life. One
> category consists of bodily diseases—say, leprosy, tuberculosis, or
> cancer—which, by rendering imperfect the functioning of the human
> body as a machine, produce difficulties in social adaptation. In con-
> trast to the first, the second category is characterized by difficulties in
> social adaptation not attributable to malfunctioning machinery but
> "caused" rather by the purposes the machine was made to serve by
> those who built it (e.g., parents, society, or by those who use it, i.e.,
> individuals).[8]

But then, since he treats instances belonging to the second category as
"counterfeit illnesses," Szasz obviously believes that it's a conceptual
mistake to catalogue as illness such disabilities as hysteria and
neurosis. He is right, of course, in holding that Freud revised the
concept of illness. But there are absolutely no conceptual objections to
extending that or any concept where it proves systematically useful to

change the classification of things. It is one thing to object to the change—it is conceptually as respectable to resist change as to endorse it—but doing either cannot, as such, be a mistake. Also, contrary to Szasz's insistence, there is every reason to believe that at least some who are thought to be suffering from mental illness are not shamming, malingering, or imitating admissible patterns of illness; they are simply victimized, actually incapable of "correcting" their behavior or states of mind by any straightforward choice. Their disability is not merely maladaptation but a certain kind of incapacity to adapt. Why should this be denied in the face of the evidence? In a word, Szasz is flatly mistaken about the facts: as in his discussion of malingering, which psychiatrists have badly confused, treating the imitation of illness as an illness itself (as he points out), it is clear that Szasz thinks that those who are said to be mentally ill have, for reasons bearing on a shift in the rules of social behavior, deliberately chosen to play the ill role.[9] Once this prejudice is exposed, there is no reason to resist the extension.

Nevertheless, where one such extension is plausible, others are as well, depending on our ingenuity and explanatory purposes. Since the concept of illness is distinctly normative, however we extend it or whatever adjustments we make in its criteria, we are likely to sanction some departure from previously acceptable norms of health. There are, inevitably, practical consequences entailed. For instance, to classify neurosis as an illness is to mobilize an already institutional habit of care, and to classify it as a sort of personal and social maladaptation is to disengage medicine and to invite a distinct sort of appreciation. It is notorious how much heat has been generated as to whether those coming for aid are "patients" or "clients" and as to whether those providing aid are "treating" or "counselling." Also, since even the explanatory function of medicine serves ulterior practical concerns about organizing the care of people victimized or incapacitated in various ways, it is really hopeless to argue that it is flatly correct or incorrect to classify mental illness as genuine illness. The classification of animals can be "corrected," within limits that tolerate the gradation of one species into another, precisely because evolutionary and genetic explanations are the principal concern of the relevant sciences. But there is no comparable concern in medicine. The convenience, the unity, and the effectiveness of professionalized forms of *aid* are decisive; the relevant forms of explanation only subserve those ends.

Of course, neurosis is only one candidate for classification as an illness, under some extended notion. It may be asked, conceding disability, victimization, and prospects of recovery, whether such phenomena as amnesia, stuttering, obesity, diabetes, baldness, sexual impotence, allergies, phobias, aphasias, kleptomania, schizophrenia, homosexuality, depression, autism, psychopathy, genetic predisposition to criminality, reading disabilities, tics, fatigue, aging, alcoholism, addiction, insomnia, and the like may fairly and usefully be classified as illnesses or disorders of some sort. To consider the extension is to admit the impossibility of providing any single model of illness to cover such phenomena. Also, to appreciate how the concept may be extended is to appreciate the reasonableness, at times, of resisting or even overturning such extensions. A good many clinical psychologists, in fact, tend to construe certain psychiatric disorders as personal or social maladjustments. Obviously, incapacities like stupidity, chronically poor judgment, lack of manual dexterity, poor memory, impressionability, weakness of character, low intelligence, and literal-mindedness would not normally be viewed as forms of illness; and yet, being disabilities, they may be corrigible or at least their undesirable consequences may be offset by some sort of professional assistance. Under imaginable circumstances, linked for example to eugenic breeding, on "professional" grounds, it is quite easy to see how the argument would go, if certain incapacities were to be viewed as medically significant.

There are at least two distinctions that confirm the inherent informality of medical norms. One concerns homeostasis, the best-known model of physical health.[10] On the homeostatic view, the body is in a state of health when its metabolic processes are functioning in such a way as to maintain a stable and balanced internal environment. The trouble is that it is fair to say that the body functions homeostatically when it is ill and dying and that it may function in an admirably homeostatic way even when the system is seriously defective, as when a human being lives a nearly vegetative life for years. The question to be faced is, precisely, *which* homeostatic norm should we prefer, and why? Construe a certain measure of intelligence, as determined by the condition of the brain, as minimally necessary for health; brains that cannot provide a physical basis for such intelligence will be judged medically defective. Construe a certain measure of longevity, as determined by the condition of the body, as necessary for normal health; bodies functioning adequately on one homeostatic model will then be judged defective on another. There is no way to avoid such choices.

But behind them, there lurks a greater puzzle. Consider that a postman has as his proper function the delivery of mail to the right people, at the right time, in the right way. The vacuity of the observation is benign enough, since, in any routinized society, what it is to deliver mail correctly is easy enough to specify: one merely consults acceptable practice. To know the postman's function in detail is to know the institutional practices that define his role; there is nothing else to consult. There are no heavenly or natural norms of postmanship by which to judge the work of earthly postmen.

The trouble is that, although to know the norms of postmanship, one need consult only the practices of a society, we are rather unwilling to regard the norms of medicine in a similar way. Presumably, medicine addresses itself not only to the causes and cures of what society admits as maladies, but also to discovering the very norms of health by reference to which such maladies are correctly so characterized. The question remains whether and in what sense such discoveries can be made.

There is no logically defensible way, it seems, in which to discover the functions of man. The functions of artifacts and offices are not discovered; there are intentional objectives, in accord with which artifacts are made and institutions arranged. To invent the one is to invent the other. What occurs in nature may be assigned a function, but only in terms of the interests and activities of men. The claim that God created man in His image is a canny intuition about what is needed: man was *made* to function thus and so. To give up such claims, however, is to deny that science is capable of discovering the natural function of anything.

Still, the loss is hardly a serious one. As already argued, medicine is a prudential art. The details of the relevant sciences are not in the least affected by their reinterpretation in functional terms. The only question that arises, admittedly of a profound importance socially, concerns the competence, the scope, the responsibility, the social consequences of medical practice as it is defined and directed. There is no way to settle that appraisal once and for all: its resolution cannot be convincingly separated from a reasoned review of the entire battery of social services that particular communities provide.

Beyond this, it needs to be remarked that the practice of medicine, notably psychiatry, is committed to a bifocal model of health. On the one hand, schemata of functional homeostasis are assigned to particular, interlocking systems within the body, in accord with determinate prudential requirements; and on the other, norms of human happiness, maturity, self-realization, and the like are regularly posited, in accord with which a broader range of clinical disabilities may be specified.[11] The first are no more tendentious than our prudential concerns; the second are decidedly tendentious, committed as they are to some favored view of the proper function of man. Gradually, of course, our technological skills affect the conception of the boundaries of medicine as they do the competence of every professional group. In fact, the rationale for altering the scope of medicine lies largely with the rationale for dividing responsibility for all the services a society provides. Even where physical medicine is most conservative, potentially radical changes in environment and technology may affect our conception of the conditions of health and illness. It is obvious that to construe neurosis, suicidal attempts, homosexuality, psychopathy as forms of illness is impossible without reference to the norms of well-being; but it is not quite so obvious that to construe forms of aging, levels of vigor, and the like as clinical deficiencies is also impossible without reference to the same norms of happiness and well-being.

It is in this sense that medicine is to be understood as a purely instrumental discipline subject to all the vagaries of ideological pressure. The minima of health are barely tendentious, since every viable society depends on the continued life and physical strength of its people. There is no important people, however, that has not professionalized medicine and there is none that has ever restricted medicine to such minima. Inevitably, medicine relates the norms of health to the dominant interests of an ongoing society; also, increasingly, to the properties of the environment, internal as well as external, that is itself increasingly the product of man's technology and exploitation.[12] The admitted conservatism of medicine misleads us into thinking that the norms of heath are open, in some sense, to scientific discovery. The truth is that no discovery is needed, since medicine is a form of prudence concerned with the least changeable, but not unchanging, stratum of our cultural life. But then, precisely, it cannot provide a model for the direction of any other of our cultural concerns.

Notes

1. The most sustained attack on the "myth" of mental illness is afforded by Thomas S. Szasz, *The Myth of Mental Illness* (New York: Hoeber-Harper, 1961). See also Joseph Margolis, *Psychotherapy and Morality* (New York: Random House, 1966), for a detailed criticism of Szasz's views. For a general account of health and illness, see H. Tristram Engelhardt, Jr., "The Concepts of Health and Disease," in *Philosophy and Medicine*, Vol. I (Dordrecht: D. Reidel, 1974). Of particular interest is Engelhardt's reference to Alvan Feinstein's concept of "lanthanic diseases," that is, of disease syndromes that may obtain without a person's being ill; see *Clinical Judgment* (Baltimore: Williams and Wilkins, 1967).

2. Homosexuality has very recently been recommended for removal as an illness from the American Psychiatric Association's *Diagnostic and Statistical Manual of Mental Disorders* (DSM-II), 3rd. ed. (Washington: American Psychiatric Association, 1968); section 302. Still, the APA has not construed homosexuality as normal but rather as a "sexual

orientation disturbance": it remains a diagnostic category but not, as such, a category of mental illness. See *The New York Times*, 16 December 1973, pp. 1, 25. The ruling,however, is anomalous, because it seems to depend on whether homosexuality may still be construed as a "disorder" without being an "illness," or whether it is a disorder only if it is viewed by homosexuals themselves as a sort of "subjective distress"; furthermore, it seems to depend on some implied model of normality, with respect to which it is defective or deficient even if homosexuals are neither ill nor disturbed by their condition. But in the view of Dr. Robert L. Spitzer, head of the APA Task Force on Nomenclature and Statistics and the principal author of the revision, "normal and abnormal are, strictly speaking, not psychiatric terms," a thesis which threatens all the distinctions of the *Manual.* See *The New York Times*, 23 December 1973, p. E5; also, *APA Monitor*, February 1974, pp. 1, 9; and Robert J. Stadler et al., "A Symposium: Should Homosexuality Be in the APA Nomenclature?" *American Journal of Psychiatry* 130(1973): 1207-16. But without some reasoned defense of normality, the entire issue, as well as a good many more identified in the *Manual*, are left utterly without a conceptual anchor.

3. See Philip Rieff, *Freud, The Mind of the Moralist* (New York, Viking, 1959).

4. See Antony Flew, *Evolutionary Ethics* (London: Macmillan, 1967).

5. But see René Dubos, *Mirage of Health* (New York: Harper and Row, 1959), Ch. 2, for some extraordinary instances of physiological variations among the peoples of the world that bear on survival but that, under altered circumstances, would surely count as simple patterns of illness or medical defect. Perhaps the most notable instance is that of sickle-cell anemia, which confers immunity to malaria, and which apparently "serves" to provide a relatively stable population under the conditions of Central African life.

6. See Nicholas N. Kittrie, *The Right to be Different* (Baltimore: Johns Hopkins Press, 1971); Thomas S. Szasz, *The Myth of Mental Illness;* Erving Goffman, *Asylums* (Garden City: Anchor Books, 1961).

7. See Szasz, *The Myth of Mental Illness*, and his *The Manufacture of Madness* (New York: Harper and Row, 1970). For a sense of the ease with which portions of the psychiatric tradition, particularly under the influence of psychoanalysis, move from the mental illness of individuals to the mental illness of societies, see Martin Birnbach, *Neo-Freudian Social Philosophy* (Stanford: Stanford University Press, 1961).

8. *The Myth of Mental Illness*, Ch. 2. See also Margolis, *Psychotherapy and Morality.*

9. *The Myth of Mental Illness*, Chs. 6, 15.

10. See Walter Bradford Cannon, *The Wisdom of the Body* (New York: W. W. Norton, 1942); compare, also, the related concept of stress, in Hans Selye, *The Stress of Life* (New York: McGraw-Hill, 1956).

11. See Marie Jahoda, *Current Concepts of Positive Mental Health* (New York: Basic, 1958). Failure to acknowledge the role of prudential norms and norms of happiness in the medical context misleads us into supposing that "disease" is a purely descriptive category, not a normative one.

12. See Dubos, *Mirage of Health.*

8

Insanity

Insanity, in its ordinary sense, signifies a condition of being unsound or unhealthy in the mind. Hence, to judge someone to be insane is, inevitably, to raise questions of custodial care and of the protection of the public. For that reason alone, the question is an extremely sensitive one. But there are other considerations. For one thing, insanity is often said to be a legal rather than a medical category; or, contrarily, a medical rather than a legal category. For another, ascriptions of mental health and mental illness, on which the judgment of insanity usually depends, are open to deep quarrel about whether we are able, as medical scientists, to discover the norms of thinking, emotional response, and behavior proper to human nature itself. For a third, being characterized as insane is stigmatic, sometimes more stigmatic than the charge of being a criminal; it raises, therefore, the issue of how, fairly, to treat a person so judged.

There are a great many detailed questions that may be posed about insanity, bearing particularly on responsibility and extenuating excuses. For instance, under what conditions may insanity count as a legal or moral defense for behavior otherwise legally liable or liable to moral censure? What, if it is a valid defense, may be the precise respect in which insanity mitigates or eliminates blame (for instance, because of a lack of knowledge or appreciation of right and wrong, ethical and/or legal, or of right and wrong under the circumstances, or because of a lack of self-control over one's action with or without the attendant appreciation, or because of some more pervasive illness that mitigates or debars responsibility)? Does insanity as such or insanity embodied in a more general condition count as a defense (for instance, as when one is provoked into involuntary action, in a general state of mental illness or mental deficiency, or as in acting in what is presumed to be self-defense, in a comparable state of mental illness or deficiency)? What may we take "insanity" to cover and are the insane ever legally or morally responsible, or, if so, under what conditions? Are insanity, legal liability, and conviction of a crime compatible, or, if so, may the insane justifiably be punished or only treated or restrained or "protected," or are such theoretical distinctions significantly different with respect to civil rights and personal freedom? Is there a formulable and straightforward criterion of insanity, particularly bearing on legal liability? Is so-called insanity socially induced or the result of forces over which individuals cannot be expected to have sufficient control? Is insanity no more than a purely conventional category corresponding to the institutionalized interests of a given society?

Conceptually, insanity obliges us to bring together our speculations about the normal functioning of human beings; for, on any view, the insane lack some capacity of rational judgment and/or rational self-control thought to be minimally normal, and constitute, because of that, a danger to themselves and/or to the public at large. This provides the theoretical basis for detecting insanity and defending society's right and obligation to control and care for the insane. In the legal context, the thesis is said to derive from the *parens patriae* doctrine, that the King has the care of his people, acting in a parental role, and that non-criminal proceedings concerning such matters as custodial care, grooming and socializing individuals, particularly where "physical, mental, or social shortcomings" are involved, derive from the King's power or its constitutional surrogates.[1] Practically, the admission of insanity provides an important basis for the direction and control of portions of a society.

Insanity, however, is a delicately balanced notion. For instance, it is quite clear that one may be liable to sanction or blame or constraint, ethically, legally, politically, both when one is and when one is not insane. It is also clear that one may be judged insane, for instance, legally, without being mentally ill, as in arguments of temporary insanity or where medical and legal distinctions fail to converge; and one may be mentally ill though not insane. Crime, illness, and insanity constitute divergent, even if sometimes overlapping, departures from the prudentially prescribed patterns of normal or acceptable behavior supported by a given society. To judge a person insane is to render a verdict or a verdict-like judgment. In the legal context, it is to render a distinctly legal verdict, normally but not necessarily informed by medical testimony, sometimes but sometimes not based on the appraisal of criminal behavior. For instance, a person certified as insane on medical testimony, in accord with legal procedures, may be committed custodially though he has committed no crime; and where a putative crime has been committed, a merely medical judgment of insanity is not as such legally decisive, as, for example, not entailing acquittal. Both the medical and the legal judgment of insanity, however, are concerned with an actual breach or a disposition toward breaching acceptable patterns of behavior, normally entailing culpability of some sort, not necessarily criminal. The medical judgment is concerned more with prudential interests bearing on the use of one's body and person; the legal, the protection of personal and institutional interests against the encroachment of others.

As a legal or ethical defense, insanity is a thoroughly conventional and conservative plea.[2] This holds for defenses in accord both with the famous M'Naghten rule[3] and the equally famous, but perhaps misleading, rule of "irresistible impulse."[4] The M'Naghten rule, whatever its vagueness and equivocation may obscure, is nothing but an extension of an implicit rule of excuses that operates, within variable constraints, in standard legal and ethical contexts, precisely where mental illness or insanity is not at stake. For instance, if a child or mental defective were judged not to appreciate the difference between right and wrong, as institutionally embodied, and/or the difference as applied to that child's or defective's specific behavior, it is very likely that what might otherwise have been judged a crime would be judged to be an act committed by someone relevantly incompetent. Some form of constraint or custodial care might well be indicated, in lieu of punishment, but the excuse of incompetence and the attendant mitigation or waiver of culpability form an essential part of the application of rules of conduct under any administration that concedes the relevance of a defendant's mental state. We see this already in the admissible excuse that someone was ignorant of what he did or of the circumstances in which he acted, without involving insanity or incompetence regarding right and wrong. The M'Naghten rule simply holds

> that to establish a defense on the ground of insanity, it must be clearly proved that, at the time of the committing of the act, the party accused was laboring under such a defect of reason, from disease of the mind, as not to know the nature and quality of the act he was doing; or if he did know it, that he did not know he was doing what was wrong,

which assigns the cause justifying the conventional excuse to a "disease of the mind."

Also, of course, the defense does not in the least concern the inherent difficulty of fixing the defendant's mental condition. *If* legal institutions presuppose informed and rational agents, it is inconceivable that incompetence with respect to right and wrong would not count as a defense against charges of culpability. The only quarrelsome matter concerns which manifestations of mental illness count as a legally valid instance of insanity. Obviously, ignorance with respect to the law, ignorance regarding what is legally right and wrong, is normally not a mitigating consideration, certainly not one that indicates insanity or mental illness. Also, some forms of mental illness do not entail incompetence regarding right and wrong, for instance, the phobias; and some forms of mental illness that might produce incompetence might not actually have done so in the circumstances given. Finally, the M'Naghten plea need not be the sole basis on which insanity because of mental illness may be offered in defense.[5]

If the argument holds for the M'Naghten rule, its counterpart will have to be conceded for the rule of "irresistible impulse"—more accurately, the rule that holds that acquittal may be directed on the grounds of a defendant's incapacity to control his behavior by reason of insanity, not characteristically restricted to a mere impulse. Again, the rule is an extension of an essential rule of standard excuses, namely, that responsible agents are agents capable not only of appreciating the distinction between right and wrong but of acting deliberately and intentionally in accord with that distinction. For instance, if a man were coerced, say, under the threat of death, into acting contrary to what he rightly believed to be right conduct, it is very likely that he would not be held culpable, or not in the full degree, for what he did. Here, there is no implication of illness or of incompetence regarding right and wrong. There is, in fact, no implication that our defendant was actually unable to refuse to act as he was forced to act, only that the price of resisting was too great to expect him to pay. The upshot is that if one may be said not to be able to control or direct his behavior under such circumstances, it is only a debatable though an important detail whether and to what extent to concede that one may be incapable of controlling or directing his behavior for reason of mental illness —whether temporarily or as a general or recurrent condition. The "irresistible impulse" rule simply posits that the agent "by reason of the duress of such mental disease, . . . [has] so far lost the power to choose between the right and wrong, and to avoid doing the act in question, . . . that his free agency was at the time destroyed."

Hence, both the M'Naghten rule and the "irresistible impulse" rule are perfectly conventional ethical and legal defenses, once it is supposed that the agent's state of mind is relevant to his defense and empirically accessible. The fact is that the issue of cognitive and volitional competence is bound to arise, with or without regard to the question of mental disease or defect. There are no mental factors that affect one's acts, that bear on justification, excuse, responsibility, liability, and culpability, except the factors just mentioned. Hence, the M'Naghten rule and the "irresistible impulse" rule cannot convincingly be eliminated, though there is no question that they may be improved. This is why the legal defense of insanity is just the defense it is: it maintains that the agent, at the time of action, was mentally ill and that that condition caused a legally relevant cognitive or volitional incapacity with respect to an otherwise criminal act.

It ought to be noticed, however, that it is quite impossible to defend an agent on a criminal charge solely on the grounds of mental illness. This is the apparent strategy of the so-called Durham rule, which holds that an agent cannot be held "criminally responsible if his unlawful act is the product of mental disease or mental defect."[6] In fact, by collapsing distinctions altogether, some theorists, Philip Roche, for instance, have construed crime as nothing more than a manifestation of mental illness. "Crime," Roche says, "is a disturbance of communication, hence a form of mental illness."[7] But, of course, the thesis is extraordinarily naive in failing to take into account the historical contingencies of what is labeled a crime and the problematic status of specifications of illness and disease.

The trouble is that the Durham rule provides no rule at all with respect to which criminal responsibility can be assessed, unless, by some adjustment, it can be taken to draw us back to the M'Naghten rule and the "irresistible impulse" rule or to some analogous modification of existing laws. Those rules do not entail a faculty psychology:

they require only that we acknowledge that the grounds of the insanity plea concern cognitive and volitional defects. More hospitably construed, the Durham rule is the determin*able* formula for determin*ate* insanity defenses like that of the M'Naghten rule and/or for defenses in terms of diminished responsibility due to mental illness short of insanity. There are circumstances, it should be noted, in which mental illness may be construed as a defense or mitigating factor with respect to otherwise criminal action, where, precisely, the insanity plea is obviated. For instance, if a homicide were committed during an epileptic seizure, the act might be judged to be involuntary, the condition contributing, though the agent might not be judged insane or mentally defective. Alternatively, a defense based on self-defense might be supported even where the objective facts fail to bear the claim out, if the agent were, say, unduly fearful or the like because of mental illness or mental defect, without yet being insane.

The insanity plea is worrisome because it requires a close consideration of the mental state of agents at the time of their action. This appears to allow justice to be either manipulated because of the imprecision involved in characterizing mental states or delivered into the hands of medical specialists. Neither charge is as readily dismissed as advocates of the relevance of psychological states would insist. Alleged insanity is often said to be a borderline and temporary phenomenon and extremely difficult to confirm (the defense of Jack Ruby may be mentioned here).[8] Also, the familiar pattern of adversary psychiatrists failing to agree on actual classification, clearly linked to defense and prosecution, or not even agreed on the extension of "mental illness," suggests that something less than medical expertise is often decisive. Still, the verdict and the judgment ultimately remain legal matters and the argument for expert testimony regarding mental states cannot be discredited, once it is admitted that information about such states is pertinent and that a developing science specializing in the analysis required is at hand.

In fact, provision has always been made, in the criminal law, for psychological considerations. It is true that this has normally been presumed not to require an independent examination of the agent's actual mental state, in the sense bearing on the insanity defense, on the grounds that agents were presumed rational and their actions presumed to yield conclusive evidence of their probable intent. Ironically, the application of the doctrine of *mens rea* (guilty mind) effectively precluded attention to actual psychological factors now deemed relevant to the insanity defense and other defenses, as of diminished responsibility and provocation.[9] But since criminal action is defined as voluntary and the developing behavioral sciences have shown the need to discount the voluntary in all sorts of ways that require attention to the agent's actual mental state, the conceptual provision has, by our own time, begun to be pressed into an entirely new role. The presumed competence and concerns of the reasonable man, opposed by the evil intent of the criminal (the heart of the *mens rea* doctrine), have been challenged by the development of psychiatry and allied disciplines. In this, psychiatrists have often gone too far. In opposing the *mens rea* doctrine, they have often attacked the so-called thesis of free will, substituting a determinism in the name of science; but they have, also, typically failed to understand the conceptual issues involved, in particular, that the relevant denial of voluntary control in given instances entails the capacity for such control in other imaginable instances.[10] Not only have actual mental states gained an increased relevance in criminal cases, but the assumed fixity of the ethical and prudential interests of reasonable men, embodied in the *mens rea* doctrine, has been independently undermined.

The import of these considerations is quite straightforward. The presumption of unqualified voluntary control cannot be maintained in the face of empirical findings, even where insanity is disallowed.[11] And the presumption of fixed prudential, ethical, and legal values cannot be maintained in the face not only of radically competing convictions but also of the conceptual requirements of the thesis. The defeasibility of voluntary control does not entail a determinism that eliminates responsibility and culpability. And the partisan nature of normative conventions does not entail the inappropriateness of criminal and similar proceedings.

In fact, the irony is that the apparently humane intention of the insanity defense has been all but thwarted, since the custodial model for managing those judged insane normally involves indefinitely extended commitment, as opposed to set terms of imprisonment, the loss of effective means of appeal, and conditions of life not always significantly different from those of imprisonment itself. It is clear that insanity, relevantly, entails acquittal, but not necessarily freedom, since a danger to self or society may always be argued. From this point of view, the distinction between punishment and custodial commitment is purely verbal, entirely at the service of an enforcing society bent on preserving its own values, at a price and by alternative means if available.[12] In fact, there is no formulable basis, except in terms of alleged intent and comforting ideology, for distinguishing between retribution short of capital punishment or the like, deterrence, rehabilitation, reeducation, protective confinement, custodial commitment, or treatment. But this is precisely what we should expect: a battery of doctrinally varied devices for maximizing conformity to a society's norms and for minimizing internal threats to their continuity.

In principle, then, insanity is a disposition to behave contrary to one's own presumed prudential interests and/or contrary to those of society at large, in ways caused by mental illness or mental defect, particularly where such behavior entails an incapacity to distinguish between right and wrong or between prudential advantages and disadvantages and/or an incapacity to control one's own behavior. The prospect of raising the insanity plea obtains only when some individual's behavior appears to violate the legal, political, or moral norms of the society in ways that render that person otherwise liable to blame, sanction, constraint, punishment, or penalty. The insanity defense argues that the causes of the offending behavior relevantly depend on the mental illness or defect of the person so charged. But the concept of illness or defect on which the defense rests—and we must not suppose that because it is construed as a defense, the insanity plea is favorable to the interests of the defendant—embodies the very norms of ethically, legally or politically acceptable conduct that allegedly have been violated.[13] In this sense, the insanity defense cannot but be an instrument for maximizing conformity to the very norms in question.

We should not conclude from this alone, however, that the underlying conception of illness and insanity is untenable; it does mean that the insanity defense concerns a degree of tolerance and flexibility respecting what may be required of a population vis-à-vis certain favored behavioral objectives. Furthermore, invoking the *parens patriae* doctrine where no crime or overt act obtains, it is obvious that the state may exert its power in an even more general way to enforce conformity and restrict the liberty of those who do not conform.[14] Clearly, the success with which judgments of insanity may be kept from serving merely conformist objectives depends jointly on the precision with which the relevant distinctions regarding mental illness or defect may be made and neutrally justified and the care with which those duly judged insane may be protected against purely penal uses of otherwise custodial and therapeutic institutions.[15]

By the same token, the detection and care of the insane is an inescapable concern of every human society; for, once it is admitted that men may act contrary to their own prudential interests, not as a result of deliberation or rational choice, it is simply inconsistent to provide constraints on the practice of medicine and the law, on the care and rearing of the young, on the treatment of the unborn fetus and future unborn generations, and to disregard, at the same time, the care of those who, because of mental illness, constitute a danger to themselves and others. The category of insanity is conceptually required by those who concern themselves with crime and illness. The three distinctions concern, in different but complementary ways, the deployment of our prudential interests. So, if it is a mistake to subsume crime under the heading of mental illness, tantamount to subsuming the criminal law under medicine, it is also a mistake to subsume insanity under the heading of deviance, heresy, nonconformity, delinquency, or crime.

Both conceptions confuse freedom and causality. The all-embracing therapeutic thesis inclines toward the view that no one can justifiably be considered responsible for so-called criminal acts, the act itself being the result of causal forces, including internal forces, over which one has no control. The all-embracing conformity thesis inclines toward the view that one is always capable of behaving or not behaving in accord with socially assigned roles, insane and mentally ill behavior being, whether usefully or not, the implied choice of the apparent patient. In principle, the difference between criminal and insane acts depends on the capacity to distinguish right and wrong appropriately and on the capacity to control one's own behavior: the criminal exhibits both capacities and the insane, either not one or not the other or neither.[16] In any case, the therapeutic thesis assumes that physicians and therapists exercise a measure of choice; and the conformist thesis cannot deny the empirical evidence regarding our cognitive and volitional capacities. In this sense, it is impossible to defend the reduction of crime to mental illness or of mental illness and insanity to mere nonconformity, or, as some have argued, to a conformist nonconformity. But to say this much is to concede that the force of the argument depends on the objectivity with which the norms of crime and illness may actually be provided. That is an altogether fair and independent question. In the present context, it is sufficient to observe that insanity is a concept parasitic on those concepts.

A competent society cannot but have as its permanent concern the care of the unborn, the young, the infirm, the deviant, the delinquent, the insane, the indigent, the defective, the weak, the inept, the inferior, the aged, and the dying. To say so is not to say that the treatment of one such group can be justifiably construed in terms of the treatment of another or, indeed, to say what the justifiable treatment of any group might be. The question insanity poses is not merely that of who is and who is not insane, and what decides the issue, but the question of what interests human societies may reasonably be supposed to pursue, in virtue of which competing criteria of insanity and of the treatment of the insane may be objectively appraised. As we now understand the matter, judgments of insanity are either legal or medical judgments, where the expertise regarding incapacity is medical and the expertise regarding crime and danger to self and society is legal. Joining these distinctions, however, raises grave problems for public policy, namely, whether and why the incapacities in question are to be medically ascertained and whether and why the dangers alleged are to be examined under the criminal law or without regard to due process.

In principle, insanity is a disorder of the prudential capacities of men. Therein lies the source of its social ambiguity. For it is entirely possible, as in suicide, war, even eccentric modes of life, to repudiate the usual prudential objectives, without in the least being irrational or incapacitated. But two characteristic sorts of confusion intrude: one, where the rationally qualified preference of deviant policies and objectives is construed as a sort of prudential incapacity; the other, where deviant behavior or the disposition to behave deviantly is construed as threatening.

Being a disorder of prudence, insanity is a civil concern first and foremost. It cannot be construed as falling within the sole competence of political, educational, medical, legal, or therapeutic professionals. For that very reason, it is impossible to free the use of the category from serving a society's need to insure a measure of conformity. What the concept of insanity explicates, therefore, is the interlocking complexity of society itself: that commitment to certain objectives reasonably entails commitment to others and that such commitments cannot but be hierarchically ordered. In the nature of the case, institutions regarding the management of insanity cannot but be fitted to whatever may be provided for the management of illness and crime. And that is quite enough, particularly where sensitive objectives are affected, to insure the partisan use of the distinction itself.[17]

Wherever the *prima facie* rationality of conforming to prudential objectives is converted into an inflexible constraint and wherever determinable objectives are authoritatively interpreted as requiring determinate forms of behavior, particularly of a political, moral, or legal nature, the threat of doctrinal manipulation is paramount. But to say that the threat is paramount is only to attend to the accidents of the social arena; in reality, the very concept of insanity, construed both in terms of overt acts and dispositions to act, presupposes an entire network of legitimate constraints, linking prudential and ulterior concerns, that cannot possibly be validated in ways that would not provide for such manipulation.

Notes

1. See Nicholas N. Kittrie, *The Right to be Different* (Baltimore: Johns Hopkins Press, 1971), Ch. 1.

2. This line of argument is relentlessly pursued by Thomas S. Szasz, *The Myth of Mental Illness* (New York: Hoeber-Harper, 1961). Unfortunately, although his exposure of the social abuse of the *institution* of mental illness is admirable, he rests his case on a dubious analysis of the concept of illness itself. In a later book that presupposes the argument of this one, *The Manufacture of Madness* (New York: Harper and Row, 1970), Szasz argues that "the concept of mental illness is analogous to that of witchcraft" and "serves the same social function" (Introduction), namely, to isolate and control heretics, social deviants, and the like. The social abuses that are challenged are impressive enough, but the oversimplification is unfortunate: mental illness is not altogether analogous to witchcraft (it is analogous in important respects to physical illness), and insanity is not mere deviance or socially undesirable heresy.

3. Full references to the text of the M'Naghten rule, given below, may be found in Abraham S. Goldstein, *The Insanity Defense* (New Haven: Yale University Press, 1967). See also Manfred S. Guttmacher, *The Role of Psychiatry in Law* (Springfield: Charles C. Thomas, 1968) and Justine W. Polier, *The Rule of Law and the Role of Psychiatry* (Baltimore: Johns Hopkins University Press, 1968).

4. See Goldstein, *The Insanity Defense,* for the text cited below.

5. Goldstein reports that, as of 1967, it was the "sole formula used by the courts of thirty states (and of Great Britain) to define insanity for the jury," *The Insanity Defense,* p. 45.

6. Durham v. United States, 214 F. 2d 862 (D.C. Cir. 1954), *overruled,* United States v. Brawner, Crim. No. 22, 714 (D.C. Cir., June 23, 1972).

7. Philip Q. Roche, *The Criminal Mind* (New York: Farrar, Strauss, and Cudahy, 1958), p. 241. See Antony Flew, *Crime or Disease?* (New York: Harper and Row, 1973).

8. See Guttmacher, *The Role of Psychiatry in Law.*

9. See H. L. A. Hart, "Negligence, *Mens Rea,* and Criminal Responsibility," in *Oxford Essays in Jurisprudence,* ed. A. G. Guest (New York: Oxford University Press, 1961).

10. See, for example, Franz Alexander and Hugo Staub, *The Criminal, the Judge, and the Public* (Glencoe: Free Press, 1956); also, the statement of Ernest Jones, cited in Guttmacher, *The Role of Psychiatry in Law,* p. 29. See also Joseph Margolis, *Psychotherapy and Morality* (New York: Random House, 1966).

11. This, in fact, is one of the essential flaws of Szasz's diatribe against the doctrine of mental illness: he is persuaded, against the evidence, that the so-called mentally ill invariably, deliberately, and of their own volition, adopt the role of being ill. See *The Myth of Mental Illness,* and Margolis, *Psychotherapy and Morality.*

12. See Erving Goffman, *Asylums* (Garden City: Anchor Books, 1961); and Thomas S. Szasz, *Law, Liberty and Psychiatry* (New York: Macmillan, 1963). See also Phyllis Chesler, *Women & Madness* (Garden City: Doubleday, 1972); and Michel Foucault, *Madness & Civilization,* trans. Richard Howard (New York: Random House, 1965).

13. See Goffman, *Asylums;* and Szasz, *The Myth of Mental Illness.*

14. See Szasz, *The Manufacture of Madness.*

15. See Kittrie's attempt at a "therapeutic bill of rights," *The Right to be Different,* pp. 400-404.

16. See for further discussion Margolis, *Psychotherapy and Morality.*

17. See Szasz, *The Manufacture of Madness,* Ch. 12.

9

Perversion

Many are revolted by such sexual excesses as necrophilia and coprophilia. But the question remains, *Who* is revolted, why, and what implications may be drawn from the fact? There are bizarre sexual games described by the Marquis de Sade that conventional imaginations would never dream of independently, considering which, such imaginations typically become, first, shocked; then, titillated; eventually, bored. It is a humorous truth, furthermore, that the censor's zeal to ban pornography has always been obliged to admit that the extreme tastes of so-called perverts and sexual deviants characteristically fail to serve the "prurient interests" of the average or "normal" man, and vice versa. Whose delicacy should we favor?

The judgment that certain practices, sexual or not, are not merely perverse but perverted argues that there are practices that are demonstrably proper for the entire human race. Perversity is thought to be a defect of judgment or interest; perversion, a defect of appetite or desire and consequent gratification. Deviance may be construed either statistically or normatively: perversity is sometimes construed merely statistically or in a way minimally touched by reference to the normal; perversion is invariably linked to the abnormal, in the sense of the sick or the evil. Principally, we think of the sexual, but the perversion of hunger and thirst is not unimaginable. Although the perversion of power, primarily the desire for power, is often mentioned, the judgment involves more attenuated claims about the normal than judgments about bodily appetites, or desires (like the sexual) that are closely linked to bodily appetite. The reason is instructive. A perverted form of sexuality is thought to be one that fails to serve in the appropriate way or to conform sufficiently closely to the commonly accepted function of sexual desire; hence a sexual pervert is a person whose nature is so upset that he prefers acts or objects or ways of performing that do not serve, or are insufficiently congruent with, the function of the sexual drive itself. Presumably, the more deviant such behavior from that function, the more monstrous the perversion. But our intuitions about the function of the drive for power are understandably suspect, even if Hitler and Stalin seem readymade paradigms: they are bound to vary from ideology to ideology.

The fact is that it is not entirely easy to specify the function even of sexual desire. Is it, for instance, only designed to facilitate the reproduction of the species? If so, then the impotent, the infertile, and those beyond the age of bearing must be somewhat perverted in whatever sexual play they engage in. Since only a fraction of the population needs to be enlisted in the reproductive effort, it may be that the race is largely inclined to the perverted duplication of the essential sexual function. Also, on this view, *all* sexual play becomes suspect, since most of it cannot be consummated in the required way and whatever portion can may not have been so intended. Again, if we hold that we must now restrict the world's population, then we might quite plausibly construe all "unauthorized" sexual activity as deviant and tending toward the perverted. But if we concede that sexual play functions as a social bond and an important ingredient in sensitizing and educating human beings in general, then it may well be counterproductive to disallow any form of sexual behavior that the race finds itself markedly interested in.[1] It is even conceivable that sexual play, perhaps, by a "natural" irony, certain so-called perverted practices, may serve a distinctly nutritive or homeostatic "function." What should we say then? If the race were desperately concerned to restrict its numbers consistently with its actual appetite, deviant sexual behavior might well be taken to serve a distinctly "natural" function in deflecting our reproductive energies benignly. Finally, if it were a *function* of sexual activity to satisfy or gratify sexual desire once aroused or even to arouse sexual desire or to arouse it in order to gratify it, then variable tastes would have to be conceded, which, inevitably, would provide their own norms. There is ample evidence, in fact, that we are inadequately informed about the causal connections between arousal and sexual play and all the activities and needs that any society sustains, and that our customs are utterly tendentious in ranking the naturalness of the various forms of sexual behavior. It is obvious, for instance, that sex is politicized,[2] even in bedrooms orthodoxly committed to preserving the race with the least amount of satisfaction.

In a sense, quarrels about perversion reveal the extent to which all the details of human existence are subject to doctrinal manipulation, even a good many of the themes by which their variety is controlled. As one commentator observes, "the capacity for sexual pleasure is unevenly distributed, cannot be voluntarily acquired, and diminishes through no fault of its subject";[3] hence, despite our preoccupation with the morality of sexual behavior, what is most intimately involved in sexual desire eludes every form of moral review, being not voluntary, and what *is* subject to review is often made such because of independent considerations, as in the cruelty of sadists or in the invasion of privacy by voyeurs. So the restriction of sexual practices reflects the variable tastes of one society or another; it seems we cannot escape imposing doctrinal constraints on ourselves, even where the most spontaneous and the most automatic behavior is involved.

Sexual appetite is among the most animal of human gifts, however much it infects the whole of human life.[4] But for all that, its manifestations depend more on cultural grooming than on instinct or imprinting, and its variations, ignoring Freudian concepts of the sublimation of sexual energy, are amazingly plastic, hardly conformist. Indeed, if physiological and anatomical variations within the human race were admitted to be relevant to the specification of "normal" sexual behavior, the mere fact that there are widely distributed forms of partial hermaphroditism would effectively baffle the familiar norms of exclusive heterosexual behavior, though the evidence even here shows the decisiveness of cultural factors.[5] That such considerations are never really pursued confirms how completely sexual functions are defined in accord with "higher" doctrinal convictions.[6] In fact, given the unruly tendencies of sexual desire, sexual conformity must be the most reassuring evidence of the prospects of political conformity. It may be a causal mistake, but the regularity with which authoritarian regimes insist on the most restricted sexual conduct confirms the belief in the political importance of sex.

The politics of constraining deviance manifests itself in a number of obvious ways. First, the condemnation and disapproval of public forms of deviance entail the denial of rights and liability to legal punishment and other penalties. For example, the marriage sacrament is denied acknowledged homosexual couples; or, they may not be entitled to the same tax status as "normal" heterosexual couples. Also, it may be unlawful to form a club in which sadists and masochists meet to match their needs. It may be impossible for known "deviants" to adopt children or to hold public office, and it may be that the mere invitation to another to participate in deviant behavior constitutes a criminal offense of some seriousness. Second, the condemnation of deviance may justify a curtailment of privacy. For example, it may be supposed that circumstantial evidence regarding the intention of consenting adults to engage in "unnatural" sexual acts, or to be a party to the use of persons or materials for "prurient" interests, justifies, within otherwise fair boundaries of privacy, police raids or similar invasions. Or, parents having homosexual or bisexual preferences may be forbidden from instructing or encouraging, in the home, such preferences in their children. Third, sexual conformity is internalized through standard educational channels. The censorship of adult behavior, of course, is the principal issue; decisions regarding children and the maintenance of public order obviously introduce independent considerations. The question remains, What is sexual deviance and perversion, and on what grounds are they to be condemned, controlled, or corrected?[7]

It is an interesting fact that practices condemned as "animalistic" on the part of humans are practically or entirely non-existent among animals. For instance, human intercourse with animals is not matched by inter-species intercourse among animals themselves; and homosexuality, which one might have thought had the greatest likelihood of appearing among animals, either never occurs or is extremely marginal, appearing in unusual circumstances of strain, incipient only, never culminating in actual intercourse, or simply confused with alternative uses of behavior (as in the expression of aggression).[8] The human species appears to be the only one with a permanently sustained sexual interest, culturally reinforced, even where the usual physiological drives are noticeably absent, as among sexual neuters, and culturally elaborated in polymorphous ways going well beyond the requirements of racial reproduction. Furthermore, if we admit the standing evidence of so-called polymorphously perverse patterns among infants, confusion about gender on physical grounds, confusion about sexual roles in early family training, psychological pressures affecting sexual identity, as well as doctrinally opposed views about the defensibility of various forms of sexual deviance, it is reasonably clear that sexual deviance and perversion are distinctly, and preeminently, human phenomena. Any and all constraints about the proper use of sexual appetite and desire must rest, finally, on a theory of normative human nature. The fullest relevant model that we have is Freud's, but that model has been conclusively shown to have been pressed in the service of Freud's own moral persuasions.[9]

It is clear that if perversion were characterized in terms of deviation from, or failure to adhere to, some requirement regarding reproduction, an enormous range of sexual practices would be subject at once to the charge of perversion. "The Catholic natural law tradition," we may notice,

> accepts as self-evident that the primary purpose of sexual intercourse is procreation, and relegates as secondary such ends as fostering the mutual love of the spouses and allaying concupiscence. This conclusion is based on two propositions, that man by the use of his reason can discover God's purpose in the Universe, and that God makes known his purpose by certain "given" physical arrangements. Thus, man can deduce that the purpose of sexual activity is procreation, the continuation of the human race; and the physical arrangements God has provided may not be supplanted at man's will. We now know that not every act of *coitus* is conceptual and relational, and others relational only. But to recognize this fact is not to conclude that acts may be rendered conceptual or nonconceptual at man's will. Man is free to act only within the pattern imposed by nature.[10]

Nevertheless, the detection of natural purposes is complicated by the mere fact that we develop as cultural beings, from a certain gifted animal stock, under and only under favorable social conditions and that the forms of behavior and desire queried are irreducibly emergent as well.

There is no question that the reproduction of the race depends on intercourse, but there is no evidence that the occurrence of sexual behavior either not focused on intercourse at all or not focused on reproduction during intercourse is incompatible with, or damaging to, the reproduction of the race. Even the reproductive function itself might, in a technologically advanced society, be served as effectively by means other than by intercourse. Given that human beings have no indisputably "natural place" in physical nature, given that they are forever committed to changing, controlling, exploiting physical nature for their own culturally significant ends, it is quite conceivable that "normal" heterosexual intercourse could, in time, be assigned a vestigial reproductive role or no more than a contributory gratificational role. Would that mean that we should then be able to detect some compensating change in the naturally assigned function of intercourse, manifested, say, in "certain 'given' physical arrangements?" Or, would it mean that we must have been mistaken from the start? Apart from an appeal to fiat or revealed doctrine, there seems to be no way of answering such questions. Even if it were granted that procreation is an "important" or "prominent" function of intercourse (presumably, on prudential grounds), on what grounds could it be maintained that the function of intercourse or of sexual behavior in general is, in some timeless sense, either exclusively or inclusively or even characteristically procreative? There is no ready way of answering.

A seemingly more interesting proposal holds that the concept of sexual perversion may be developed without supposing that the connection between sex and reproduction directly bears on the definition of perversion, for example, as in Thomas Nagel's account.[11] Nagel actually goes so far as to hold that "social disapprobation or custom . . . has no bearing on the concept of sexual perversion."[12] The thesis is promising, in the first regard, since it is hopeless to resolve the question of natural function by any generally admitted objective procedure; also, since the bare reproduction of the species is hardly a serious prudential concern of the race at the present time, the normative direction of sexual desire may be defended, if it may at all, only on grounds other than that of its natural function. On the face of it, however, it seems impossible, turning to Nagel's second contention, to defend the concept of perversion without appealing either to natural function or to social disapprobation. Nagel attempts to do so by subscribing to some model of a *natural relationship between persons*, a sort of natural justice or respect.[13] The proposal has the effect of shifting our attention from the natural function of intercourse to the "natural use" of sexual relationships. In fact, on Nagel's thesis, sexual perversion need not be restricted to practices; it extends to inclinations as well. The obvious difficulty lies jointly in the attempted discovery of some natural relationship between persons, the bearing of merely sexual activity on the putative norms, moral or non-moral, of such a relationship, and the conceptual linkage by which non-conformity between the two is thought to be rightly characterized as perversion. What is essential, Nagel holds, is that "sexual desire has as its characteristic object a certain relation with something in the external world . . . usually a person."[14] The use of the terms "characteristic" and "usually" suggests a statistical interpretation of perversion, but that would hardly do. On the other hand, if they are construed normatively, then we are left with a mere analogue of the putatively natural function of intercourse; even if we replace talk about functions with talk about relations with an object, the original question of determining "unnatural," "incomplete," "unhealthy," "subhuman," "unsatisfactory," "imperfect" desires (the terms are all, in effect, used in Nagel's account) remains quite unanswered.

In criticizing Nagel's central thesis, Sara Ruddick, for one, mentions "three characteristics that distinguish better from inferior sex acts— greater pleasure, completeness, and naturalness."[15] Clearly, the first criterion must be relativized to sexual preferences; it could not possibly disqualify perversion or even provide grounds for designating particular acts as perverted. The second, which is rather difficult to formulate satisfactorily, Ruddick defines as obtaining "if each partner (1) allows himself to be 'taken over' by desire, which (2) is desire not merely for the other's body but also for _his_ desire, and (3) where each desire is occasioned by a response to the partner's desire."[16] The concept is partly derived from Sartre's formula, "The being which desires is consciousness _making itself body_,"[17] which suffers from a strongly dualistic turn of phrase but which also serves to correct a strongly dualistic turn of mind on the part of those who are not satisfactorily adjusted to the thought, or deeper feelings associated with the thought, that they possess a body. The phenomenon associated with completeness is genuine enough, but there is not the slightest reason why, as Ruddick rightly insists, incomplete sex should not be eminently pleasurable or why, against Nagel's inclination, it should be treated as perverted. Both in the general run of cases (as in "normal" heterosexuality) and in special circumstances, as in seduction, condition (3) (Nagel's contribution) does not seem to be required or even expected, let alone sufficient to establish the presence or absence of perversion. In fact, in all fairness, (3) seems idiosyncratic. The third condition, naturalness (of function), Nagel, of course, himself disqualifies; though even here, Ruddick criticizes him for confusing the _ground_ of naturalness, that sexual desire could be deployed to lead to "reproduction in normal physiological circumstances," with the _criterion_ of naturalness, congruity with such behavior. In any case, complete sex acts may, on the criteria offered, be unnatural (oral-genital intercourse, anal intercourse); and natural sexual relations may be both incomplete and unpleasurable, as, sadly, many admit. Also, it seems impossible, on the foregoing argument, to defend the concept of perversion without _some_ linkage to the reproductive function. To relativize its defense merely to prevailing practice is, in effect, to devalue the category itself; and to link it to the requirement of completeness obscures the extent to which we rely on current notions of satisfactory sex.

There is, also, the further difficulty that if it is merely linked to deviation from the natural, in the sense Nagel supplies, then perversion cannot but lose the sense of seriousness with which relevant charges are usually intended. "Unnatural" sex may be both complete and/or pleasurable and, on statistical grounds, may even facilitate the completeness and pleasurableness of "natural" sex. In fact, from this vantage, it may be argued that pornography functions as a useful adjunct for all forms of sexual activity, pleasurable, complete, or natural. Nagel thinks that homosexual relations may, on his own criterion, be complete and, though unnatural with regard to function, suitably natural in the use of personal relations—the full range of interpersonal perceptions. He stresses, therefore, that homosexuality cannot be a perversion in the same sense in which shoe-fetishism, for example, is.[18] But then, completeness is not, on Ruddick's view, incompatible with perversion, which is opposed to naturalness; and, significantly, as attested by a great number of "normal" heterosexuals with sexual problems, the failure to achieve completeness is often more a manifestation of disability than of perversion. But if this is true, then the implausibility of Nagel's thesis is patent. Also, if, say, masturbation may be complete and natural, because only one person is involved, then so may shoe-fetishism, though Nagel is inclined to emphasize the absence of "reciprocity" and the "primitive" level of such behavior.[19]

Apparently, perversion, as Nagel understands it, entails a deviation from norms of naturalness thought to be morally required of human agents or required in some analogous sense. Nagel insists that "by no means all our evaluations of persons and their activities are moral evaluations" and, "moral issues aside, it is not clear that unperverted sex is necessarily *preferable* to the perversions."[20] But it is difficult to make his argument out. If the norms are taken to be moral norms, then the thesis is clearly tendentious, given that we have no objective way to specify what is and what is not a normatively natural function.[21] If the norms are taken to be prudential, concerned with preserving the race, for instance, then the thesis is clearly false. If the norms are taken to be norms of rationality, in some sense, then, as Nagel himself admits, the thesis must face the fact that rational preference may favor perversion over "sexual perfection," that is, completeness. And if the norms are taken in some sense to constitute what it is to be essentially human or natural, then the race's sustained interest in a large range of alleged perversions would make the thesis more than doubtful. There seem to be no other viable alternatives of comparable force.

There are, in fact, no other viable alternatives *if* what is required is a defense of something like an obligation to prefer natural sex and to oppose perverted sex, in a sense suitably analogous to that of moral obligation. There is, however, another, entirely plausible, way of viewing the perversions. Grant deviation from the natural, in the standard sense or in Nagel's sense, to be a necessary condition of perversion. Then, imagine a society whose established sexual practices and tastes are sufficiently homogeneous and centered on the natural that they are inclined to find perverted sex distasteful, even disgusting. We are all, in a way, victims of publicly reinforced tastes; our spontaneous affective reactions to particular uses of food, drink, manners, clothes, and sex are, within limits, not a matter of voluntary conduct at all. There is a sense, more closely related to etiquette than to morality, in which *we ought not offend the affective dispositions of the community in which we live and move.* If it may be fixed at all, it is an "obligation" to respect the prevailing tastes of that community. Of course, it is entirely reasonable, at times, to repudiate such tastes, without failing to grasp the seriousness with which they are favored or the difficulty of giving them up.

The "obligation" not to offend prevailing taste is really a concession to tact or etiquette and, perhaps, a piece of prudential advice. To make the charge of perversion stronger—and the injunction intended—we should have to hold that we have a categorical obligation, in a moral sense or in a suitably similar sense, to adhere to natural sex. Otherwise, perversion would dwindle to what may be termed an aesthetic distinction, a distinction regarding the sensibilities of different communities. On that construction, admitting the contingency and variability of sexual tastes, the category would be nothing but an instrument of conformity.

So perversion is a distinction that we can no more resist adhering to than we can resist being culturally indoctrinated. We prefer the manners we have, not merely in the sense that we are prepared to defend them as a matter of principle but also in the sense in which our habits of affective reaction are trained to support them as a matter of psychological congruence. There is no culture without such socialized habits; and there is no system of viable and coherent human life that can be disqualified on the grounds of developing contrary to human nature. What could that possibly mean? There is a deep contingency in any cultural preference; and yet, such contingencies, like birth itself, trap and shape us as the distinctive human beings we are. It is our sense of the dilemma of culture, the contingency of customs, tastes, institutions, habits, and the need to secure them against the threat of similar contingencies, that leads us to invent all the tyrannies of public approbation. The category of perversion is merely one of the more interesting products of that sense of strain.

Deviant sex is merely that, whatever deviates markedly from the implied norms of prevailing sexual taste. Perverted sex is deviant sex viewed with regard to the criterion of the natural.[22] But if there is a weak sense, by way of an aesthetic appreciation of custom, in which we ought to respect the prevailing tastes of our society, there cannot but be a countervailing sense, not in any respect weaker, in which we ought to tolerate deviance from such norms. For, unless we could conclusively demonstrate that the tastes we favor are not merely culturally contingent but somehow linked to the normative requirements of human nature itself, we cannot but admit that our customs threaten to become arbitrary as well. In fact, the arbitrary is nothing but the contingent raised to a fixed normative function. We may, perhaps by degrees, domesticate the deviant, though we have no obligation to do so or to resist all efforts to do so. The matter is neither a moral nor a prudential one, unless accidentally. It concerns, rather, a civilized sense of the essential historical irony of human existence. Culture may be the second nature of the human animal but it is the very nature of the human person: we have only the plasticity of its alternative possibilities to govern ourselves by, as well as the rigidity of each of those possibilities, once embodied, to warn us. The deviant becomes acceptable only by providing a continuum of practices that leads from the securely approved to itself. In that way, we naturalize the unnatural. But in that way, also, and only in that way, we fix, however provisionally, what we take to be natural. In doing so, we must confess that other societies have drawn such connections differently, and will again.

The category of perversion, therefore, reflects the prudential interests of a society, displaced. One is led to think of the monstrous, the inhuman, the "animal," the "unnatural"; but behind such charges lurks a deeper seriousness about an implied threat to the fixity of our very habits of life. Where it overlaps with the insane, the criminal, and the diseased, the perverted is absorbed in explicitly prudential concerns. But where, as in sexual deviance, it is occupied only with the most limited private relationships and where the connection with these other categories is least compelling, we cannot, in the absence of an adequate theory of natural functions and natural relationships, fail to see that "perverted" tastes threaten, by proxy, our management of the insane, the criminal, and the diseased just as they threaten directly the determinate forms of our conventional desires and appetites. There is no doubt that perverted practices challenge the "higher" requirements of standard sexual moralities; but, in order to avoid the appearance of the doctrinaire, criticism is deployed in prudential terms or in terms of some norm of non-defective regard to for self and others, akin to the prudential but less than the moral. In that sense, one part of our trained tastes is made to control another.

Notes

1. See Arno Karlen, *Sexuality and Homosexuality* (New York: W. W. Norton, 1971); also Nikolaes Tinbergen, *Social Behavior in Animals with Special Reference to Vertebrates* (London: Methuen, 1965), and Konrad Lorenz, *On Aggression,* trans. Marjorie Kerr Wilson (New York: Harcourt, Brace & World, 1966).

2. The women's rights movement has provided the most forceful charges recently. The most balanced views are not restricted to the exploitation of women; see Kate Millett, *Sexual Politics* (New York: Doubleday, 1969), and Germaine Greer, *The Female Eunuch* (London: MacGibbon & Kee, 1970).

3. Sara Ruddick, "On Sexual Morality," in *Moral Problems,* ed. James Rachels (New York: Harper & Row, 1971).

4. See John Money and Anke A. Ehrhardt, *Man & Woman, Boy & Girl* (Baltimore: Johns Hopkins Press, 1973).

5. See Money and Ehrhardt, *Man & Woman, Boy & Girl.*

6. The recent reclassification of homosexuality by the American Psychiatric Association is a case in point. See references in Ch. 7.

7. There appeared recently *(New York Times Book Review,* 20 January 1974) an ad for a book titled *S-M: The Last Taboo* (New York: Grove Press, 1974), which posed the question, "SADO-MASOCHISM. Is it a dark perversion? Or part of imaginative love play?" Whatever the merit of the book, the ad manages to capture the essential conceptual quarrel.

8. The lack of confirmatory evidence of homosexuality among primates and monkeys is attested to directly by Tinbergen, Irven de Vore, Frank Beach, and Harry Harlow in interviews with Karlen. Karlen also reports the findings of John B. Calhoun, in which disturbed wild Norway rats became pansexual and were unable to discriminate among sexual partners (attacking males, females, and infants indiscriminately). See Karlen, *Sexuality and Homosexuality,* Chs. 23-24.

9. See, for example, Philip Rieff, *Freud, The Mind of the Moralist* (New York: Viking, 1959); see also Joseph Margolis, *Psychotherapy and Morality* (New York: Random House, 1966). Freud's sexual bias is explored in detail in Millet, *Sexual Politics,* "The Reaction in Ideology."

10. Norman St. John-Stevas, *Life, Death and the Law* (Bloomington: Indiana University Press, 1961), pp. 83-84—stated with tactful demurrers and doubts. It is in the spirit of this thesis that St. John-Stevas speaks of homosexuality as a distinct perversion, in contrast to "transient homosexuality" in the psychosexual development of children and adolescents and in spite of the fact that homosexuality may be "subjectively" more in accord with a homosexual's nature than heterosexuality; ibid., pp. 214-15. See also Joseph Fletcher, *Morals and Medicine* (Princeton: Princeton University Press, 1954), Ch. 3. Kar-

len, summarizing the evidence, affirms that homosexuality is certainly not genetically determined, not even physically determined (to the consternation of many homosexuals themselves); but then, human sexuality, on his view, is largely modeled by social training—even conceding such anomalous phenomena as hermaphroditism, transsexuality (as in persons believing they belong to the opposite sex), heterosexual transvestism, homosexual transvestism, masochistic transvestism, and the like; see Karlen, *Sexuality and Homosexuality*, Chs. 21-23.

11. "Sexual Perversion," *Journal of Philosophy* 66(1969): 5-17.

12. Ibid.

13. In this, Nagel follows the view of Johns Rawls, most recently (after the appearance of Nagel's article) formulated in *A Theory of Justice* (Cambridge: Harvard University Press, 1971). Nagel's view may be fairly seen as an original application of the philosophical views of Rawls and H. P. Grice ["Meaning," *The Philosophical Review* 66(1957): 377-88], informed by the theory of sexual inclination advanced by Jean-Paul Sartre [*Being and Nothingness*, trans. Hazel E. Barnes (New York: Philosophical Library, 1956), Pt. III].

14. Nagel, "Sexual Perversion."

15. Ruddick, "On Sexual Morality."

16. Ibid.

17. Sartre, *Being and Nothingness*, p. 389.

18. Nagel, "Sexual Perversion."

19. Ibid.

20. Ibid.

21. See Joseph Margolis, *Values and Conduct* (New York: Oxford University Press, 1971).

22. Michael Slote has, in an unpublished paper, "Inapplicable Concepts and Sexual Perversion," ingeniously argued that "unnatural" (also, "monster" and "perversion") is an inapplicable concept because, in effect, whatever has a biologically determinate nature has a "place in nature." The application of "unnatural" in our world is, therefore, precluded. But this reading fails to accommodate an important part of actual usage. On our own argument, the "unnatural" merely deviates from putatively natural norms, *where deviation is possible in nature*. The perverted and the monstrous are what, among unnatural things, horrify and disgust us in certain ways.

10

Inequality

Between birth and death, men fill their lives as unequals, unequal by nature, unequal by fortune, unequal by the provision of effective rights and liberties. Yet ours is an age that insists on equality: all influential ideologies sense the need to support the thesis, although it is almost completely unexamined. In fact, the only indisputable sense in which men are actually equal is just that they are born into a complex world, in which, after a short interval, they die.[1] But that sense precludes the politically serious insistence on equality: birth is the contingency that merely produces a new claimant; death, the contingency that finally excludes all claimants. Since the eighteenth century, spanning the Declaration of Independence and the United Nations Universal Declaration of Human Rights, the equality of man has been progressively conceded to be "self-evident," to be embodied in "the rights of man," "natural rights," "human rights," "inalienable rights." The claim is interesting, of course, because it is substantively vacuous and politically important at one and the same time. This needs to be explained.

It is a logical truth that "similar things must be judged in similar ways in similar respects." As R. M. Hare puts it, "the thesis that descriptive judgments are universalizable is a quite trivial thesis," for, "any singular descriptive judgment is universalizable . . . in the sense that it commits the speaker to the further proposition that anything exactly like the subject of the first judgment, or like it in relevant respects, possesses the property attributed to it in the first judgment."[2] To deny this is to contradict oneself, although to affirm it is often supposed to be to affirm a principle of justice or equality: *justice* requires that similar things be similarly treated in similar respects; *equality* requires that things that are similar are equal in the precise respect in which they are similar.[3] Thus, to call two human beings human beings or persons is to suppose that a common property may be validly attributed to them (the property of being a human being) and that, in that regard, there is no relevant difference between them: they are "equally" human beings though not necessarily equal human beings, on any scale admitted. An evil man is not less a man than a good man: as a man, he is, precisely, less than good and less good than a good man. The upshot is that *if* we have rules of any sort addressed to human beings as such, we cannot vary our judgment and treatment of them in that regard: they are equally human beings. "Justice" requires that they be equally treated *in that regard*.[4] The principle of universalizability may, then, be construed as a principle of equality. But it is a purely formal principle, has nothing to do with the defense of *any* distinctions on any scale whatsoever.

Universalizability signifies that we apply distinctions consistently for the range of all cases thought to be relevantly similar. It must, therefore, be contrasted with the policy of consistently applying these or those distinctions to a given range of cases. If a rule is to be applied consistently in all relevant cases, then the generality of the rule should be specified and defended as holding within certain boundaries, on certain conditions, in accord with certain criteria. For example, if to murder is to take another's life premeditatedly and reprehensibly, then anyone judged to have murdered will be judged to have taken another's life premeditatedly and reprehensibly; but who is to be judged to have acted thus, what grounds are to be taken as decisive, determine the limits of justified ascriptions of murder. In this sense, where men are treated similarly, they are treated "equally"; and where men are treated as relevantly dissimilar, they are treated "unequally." But these distinctions, managed in this purely formal way, cannot possibly resolve any of the well-known quarrels about the equality or inequality of men. The essential issue is, of course, how to defend the treatment of men *as relevantly different;* even differences will have to be applied consistently (that is, equally). Logic tells us that, whatever our convictions may be, we must, as rational agents, judge consistently; ideology tells us that our convictions and distinctions are just the ones that deserve to be consistently enforced.

Now, there is a comparable vacuity regarding the doctrine of human rights. Granting that human rights accrue to human beings solely because they are human, we are led to conclude that all human beings must or ought to possess those rights equally. Reading "equally" in the sense of universalizability, the thesis is obviously trivial. But even if human rights are taken to belong to human beings merely because they are human, because no further qualifications obtain, the theory remains trivial—though, perhaps, not obviously trivial. Certainly it is open to debate whether rights usually designated as human rights are or ought to be extended to all human beings or only to some appropriately selected subset of the total human population. That issue cannot be a mere quibble because *civil rights* as opposed to *human rights* are normally extended only to appropriately qualified human beings— in short, to citizens and subjects. Whatever their defense, we cannot expect to support civil and human rights on the same grounds. They presuppose different but equally general distinctions. An Englishman's civil rights accrue to him exclusively as an Englishman; a Russian's, exclusively as a Russian. But their human rights belong to both merely because they are human beings, which, redundantly, is what is meant by saying that they are inalienable. With respect to civil rights, Englishmen are to be treated equally *qua* Englishmen; "unequally," in contrast with Russians. With respect to human rights, Englishmen and Russians are to be treated equally *qua* human beings.

There is, however, a deep vacuity in assigning human rights, seen, for instance, in the Universal Declaration of the United Nations. Article 3 affirms:

Everyone has the right to life, liberty and security of person.[5]

(Article 1 holds that "All human beings are born free and equal in dignity and rights" and Article 2 disallows distinctions "such as race, color, sex, language, religion, political or other opinion, national or social origin, property, birth or other status.") But we would not support Article 3 unless we supposed human life to be worth pursuing, without prejudging what would and what wouldn't count as a worthwhile life; the "rights" accorded by Article 3 are minimally required in order to pursue any life effectively. Well, then, how could we assume life to be worth pursuing in any manner unless we supposed that human beings making the effort could reasonably expect their lives to be secure against one another through the relevant interval? Minimally, one must survive, have a personal objective of some sort, and have a measure of power over the world's resources in order to pursue any life at all. Obviously, one need not survive forever and the security of one's life need not be unconditional. All that is required is that one be accorded *some* measure of "life, liberty and security of person" conformable with some accessible range of alternative modes of life. Restrict the desirable or accessible modes: the requisite forms of life, liberty, and security of person may, correspondingly, be restricted as well. In this sense, the favored interpretation of human rights will vary from ideology to ideology. And *if* the civil rights accorded by one political community or another may be construed as the determinate forms of the human rights to which everyone is supposed to be entitled, then, obviously, criticism of a community's failure to provide proper safeguards of human rights is likely to reflect ideological quarrels about the extension of civil rights. Alternatively put, human rights cannot but be determin*able,* and civil rights, determin*ate.*

The issue is complicated by the historical contingency that, in sub- scribing to the Preamble of the Declaration, the Member States of the United Nations "pledge themselves . . . to promote respect for these rights [that is, for the enumerated rights]"; but those rights form a mixed catalogue and include not merely "human rights" but what may be called "international civil rights" as well. This is the only way to understand Article 13, for instance:

1. Everyone has the right to freedom of movement and residence within the borders of each state.
2. Everyone has the right to leave any country, including his own, and to return to his country.

Objections to recent Soviet policy regarding the emigration of Russian Jews has more to do with the "civil" rights of Article 13 than with the "human" rights of Article 3; but objections to the South African policy of *apartheid* are usually said to have more to do with the "human" rights of Article 2 than with the "civil rights" of such an article as Article 10, which provides for an impartial tribunal in determining criminal charges.

The Declaration of the Rights of Man and of Citizens, attached to the French Constitution of 1791, includes among the "sacred rights of men and of citizens" the following as the first:

> Men are born, and always continue, free and equal in respect of their rights. Civil distinctions, therefore, can be founded only on public utility.[6]

Here, the conditional entitlement of determinate civil rights is made entirely clear. Human rights vary somewhat from document to document; but by and large they include some subset of these: life, liberty, property, pursuit of happiness, security, freedom from oppression, and status as a person. Ultimately, they are all merely determinable and redundant, in the sense that they may be defensibly embodied in different and incompatible ways and in the sense that they are all entailed by the admission of the inherent worth of pursuing *some* mode of life within the usual range men are drawn to.[7]

If we put the argument about natural or human rights conditionally, then we have the least quarrelsome and the least restrictive doctrine imaginable. H. L. A. Hart says, with some flourish, "I shall advance the thesis that if there are any moral rights at all, it follows that there is at least one natural right, the equal right of all men to be free."[8] But of course, (a) moral questions concern man *qua* man; hence, (b) moral distinctions are universalizable with respect to merely being human; (c) moral concerns presuppose that life is worth pursuing in some regard or other; hence, (d) if they are to be morally effective, men must be admitted to have the right to act to advance their moral concern; but (e) that is tantamount to admitting the equal right to be free.

Hart explains that, by the right of freedom, he means

> any adult human being capable of choice (1) has the right to forbearance on the part of all others from the use of coercion or restraint against him save to hinder coercion or restraint and (2) is at liberty to do (i.e., is under no obligation to abstain from) any action which is not one coercing or restraining or designed to injure other persons.[9]

The details of "forebearance," "coercion," "restraint," "injury to others," in the absence of a demonstrably valid theory of human well-being, concern determinate civil rights rather than merely determinable human rights and a specific doctrine or ideology by which the members of a given community actually formulate those ulterior values they intend to realize by political means. Hart's prime natural right, therefore, cannot but be vacuous; although, since political agents need not be entirely rational, it is important to stress the conceptual connection between *any* relevant enterprise and the bare right of freedom. Men are equal in that, being men, they are men; they ought

to be equal in that, assuming life to be worth pursuing, men ought to be
accorded whatever rights are entailed by the pursuit of any mode of
life. Even these concessions, empty as they are, are hotly disputed
because, of course, arbitrary and irrational behavior runs deeply
through the race. But they are more important in the breach than the
observation.

On any and every scale imaginable, it is obvious that human beings
exhibit unequal ability, unequal achievement, opportunity, fortune,
benefit. They differ in longevity, health, skill, intelligence, wealth,
beauty, physical strength, and power over one another. Of course,
such inequalities are entirely compatible with the sort of equality
already canvassed: men are men, however unequal their skills and
good fortune; and, regardless of what effective rights they may be
afforded, they require the same determinable security of life and person. The point is important, for it shows at a stroke that the thesis that
men ought to be treated equally is unaffected by the mention of actual
inequalities. To be sure, it is normally not supposed that inequality
with respect to mere physical strength relevantly bears on our civil
rights, otherwise equally distributed among qualified citizens. But the
point is not always allowed for other inequalities. Reconsider Article 2
of the Universal Declaration:

> Everyone is entitled to all the rights and freedoms set forth in this
> Declaration, without distinction of any kind, such as race, color, sex,
> language, religion, political or other opinion, national or social origin,
> property, birth, or other status.

Could any state be said to have violated the *human* rights of anyone, in
refusing, under circumstances to be supplied, to accord certain subse-
quently listed rights? For example, is the differential treatment of
individuals, with regard to Article 13 (cited), invariably indefensible if
based on criteria of race, religion, political opinion, or the like? It seems
implausible to say so, in the context of Pakistani-Indian rivalries,
Russian-Chinese rivalries, and Arab-Israeli rivalries. The quarrel has
to do once again with a defensible generality. Ought men without
qualification have the freedom of movement specified by Article 13 or
ought only those who meet the constraints imposed by distinct national states have such freedom, within those states? Either view is
partisan, since it cannot be argued that the right is entailed as a
minimal condition for pursuing any usual mode of life. Article 13
actually promotes a doctrinally favored international society.

Is it proper, say, in Pakistan, to treat citizens or residents of Indian
and Pakistani origin differently, "unequally?" There is no straightfor-

ward answer, except in terms of consistency with one's own partisan convictions. *There is simply no objective basis on which to demonstrate that the equal distribution of determinate rights cannot be justifiably constrained by qualifications more restrictive than that of merely being a human being* or merely being a citizen or the like. Human rights are unconditional because they are vacuous and merely determinable. Ideological differences regarding determinate rights always remain, after all fair questions of inconsistency, incoherence, irrelevance, and arbitrariness are met. The point is obvious, ominously so, in Article XVII of the Rights of Man and of Citizens:

> The right to property being inviolable and sacred, no one ought to be deprived of it, except in cases of evident public necessity, legally ascertained, and on condition of a previous just indemnity.

Thus, the determinable human right to property may be respected even in the deprivation of a determinate civil right to property, under general conditions suitably universalized. (A suggestive analogue, here, concerns capital punishment.) The irony cannot be avoided.

In the United States, it has been generally agreed that constraints on political rights and liberties may be shown to be arbitrary or indefensible if they rest on such differences as those of sex and race. *Given* the Constitutional commitments of American life, such constraints may well function arbitrarily or indefensibly. But even there, the argument is incomplete. For instance, if there were a race-linked disease that threatened the health and stability of the country, it could hardly be maintained, assuming the prudential concerns on which the distribution of determinate rights and liberties itself depends, that the differential or "unequal" treatment of the races in that regard was inherently unfair. Obviously, the argument may be generalized for sex, intelligence, or any other distinction. By the same token, it is manifestly arbitrary to pay unequal wages for equal work performed, or to provide unequal opportunities for equal skills merely because of differences in gender or race or age or the like. Only if such differences could be shown to bear relevantly on the imposition of general constraints could they escape being judged arbitrary, on the assumption of given overriding values. The truth is that once the distribution of determinate rights is defended for particular societies set apart from others, those rights can no longer be defended solely as human rights; also, general constraints cannot be defended, except ideologically. In this sense, even the South African practice of *apartheid* may be described as conforming to the requirements of equality and human rights. This is not to endorse such a model, only to show the poverty and tendentiousness of arguments about the proper scope of determinate rights.

Of course, the issue runs deeper. There are inequalities of natural gifts, natural strengths and capacities, unbidden opportunity and fortune, that affect our lives in the most decisive ways. In the Christian tradition, such inequalities are assigned to God's providential plan: otherwise, His distribution of goods would appear unfair and indefensible. On the other hand, much that is viewed as the work of nature or chance, like hereditary or congenital dispositions, are, in principle, susceptible of some adjustment or, failing this, some human compensation. The ulterior question concerns the ethics of inequality. [10] In fact, the theory of human rights, a fortiori, the theory of civil rights, assumes that the ethics of political life requires only the provision of certain fundamental equalities. There is no viable political doctrine that requires that all men or all citizens be equal in health, longevity, beauty, talent, wealth, power, influence, intelligence, skill, or happiness, or equal in whatever degree human engineering can devise.

In one sense, then, inequality is like the condition of birth, a contingency of existence that, in the short span of a single life, can never be overtaken; no corrective program could possibly eliminate the inequalities of a given generation, no matter what adjustments it might propose for a succeeding generation; and no realistic political program could expect to concern itself with monitoring more than a very small selection of inequalities. Politically, we disregard fortuitous inequalities that we are powerless to eliminate, as well as a good many others that we suppose men not to be entitled to have politically eliminated. Needless to say, the appearance of plural systems of political rights and liberties, coupled with global differences in wealth, power, and consumption, contributes to the most incredible disparities between the citizens of different states. The condition of the African Sahel states, for example, is, at least in part, the consequence of our pious adherence to our own political rights. Nothing else could possibly account for the unforced mixture of compassion and righteousness with which well-to-do America and Europe view the impoverishment of a large part of the world.

In fact, the concept of equality is sufficiently resilient to accommodate any form of generalized inequality. [11] Reward talent, for instance, or industry, as a general rule, within a citizen population: "inequality" turns out to be a form of equality itself. The very term is equivocal: it signifies either the equality of universalizability or of some substantive generality. For instance, by Article 4 of the Universal Declaration,

> No one shall be held in slavery or servitude; slavery and the slave
> trade shall be prohibited in all their forms.

Here, not only are all human beings to be treated in the same way but
the way in which they are to be treated applies determinately to them
merely as human beings. It is entirely possible to hold that everyone
should be treated equally on the basis of his talent or intelligence or
industry and, at the same time, to hold that, as a result of *this*, substantive differences in treatment are justified.

There is no way to eliminate this possibility. It is as reasonable to
hold that men ought to be accorded equal treatment because they are
men as it is to hold that their differences sometimes justify differential
treatment. There is no other way to understand our policies affecting
the sick, the insane, the criminal any more than those affecting the
gifted, the productive, the trusted. Every political system endorses, to
some extent, both propositions. Even the *Communist Manifesto* relies on
the productivity of workers during the phase of socialist organization
in order to justify differential treatment; and, the needs of workers
during the communist phase, in order once again to justify differential
treatment.

This means that the general strategies for combatting inequalities are
basically of two sorts. There may be a third, but it could not be
compelling except among the converted, that is, the flat denial of what
appears to be an inequality. For instance, it might be held that all men
are equal "before God," that "apparent" inequalities on earth obscure
the "essential" equality of God's concern; analogously, it might be
maintained that the State treats all its subjects alike, regardless of
apparent favors. The more plausible strategies admit the usual inequalities. The first maintains that particular inequalities are wrongly
endorsed or permitted, assuming the commitment of some constitution or ideology. The second maintains that the inequalities on which
further inequalities are justified simply do not obtain.

In the United States, the best-known quarrels applying these
strategies have developed over alleged racial differences in intelligence. Comparable disputes, of course, have arisen about the relative
intelligence and capability of the sexes. Some maintain that, although
there may be measurable differences in intelligence that can be explained only on racial grounds or on the basis of the genetics of selected populations, the differentially unfavorable treatment of unfavorably endowed citizens with respect to publicly supported educational
opportunity, welfare, counselling, and the like is unjustified; these are

the partisans of the first strategy. Others maintain that it is methodologically impossible to demonstrate that measured differences in intelligence, or IQ, which may not be equated with intelligence, are due to racial traits or to genetic differences between selected populations;[12] these, of course, adhere to the second strategy. The truth is that it may be plausibly argued, on alternative ideological grounds, both that selected and measurable differences do and do not bear on the defense of politically institutionalized inequalities. The ultimate question is one of ideological adherence, though, of course, assuming a particular policy, the putative facts will be decisive. Also, the issue cannot be straightforwardly decided by establishing that given inequalities are hereditary or environmental; for, if given inequalities were environmental, it would still be possible to justify, as it would be to attack, treating citizens unequally on the basis of confirmed inequalities at the same time environmentally corrective measures were endorsed to reduce such inequalities. Also, if such compensations fail, the burden of proof eventually falls to those who continue to resist publicly endorsed inequalities.

There are, then, innumerable inequalities that may be observed among men: some, perhaps the result of natural or chance factors over which we have no control, may still be politically decisive; others, the result of human policies at least in part, we may not actually be able to correct, however politically important they may be. Normative inequalities may be condemned most reasonably where they conflict with minimal human rights. Since, however, human rights are only determinable, it is nearly impossible to demonstrate that a coherent general policy *is* actually incompatible with such rights. And normative inequalities regarding determinate rights and liberties are even more difficult to attack, except from the vantage of a competing ideology. There seem to be no other options. But to say this is to concede that, given its particular objectives, every society cannot but classify different subsets of its own citizens in politically preferential ways; also, that independent states must conduct themselves similarly vis-à-vis one another. We can, therefore, never eliminate the "unequal" treatment of men, for inequality is nothing but a general distinction unfavorably viewed from the vantage of another partisan commitment. And even we if we thought to reduce the arbitrariness of standing inequalities by assigning hitherto restricted rights to less restricted populations, we should only have substituted one ideology, however attractive and humane, for another.[13] This is not to deny that arbitrariness can be dialectically exposed. But *every* principle of division among human beings is, potentially, a rule of inequality: there is no complex society that can avoid qualifications on entitlement, and there are none that are immune to ideological complaint. The suspicions of partisans will always remain, of course. But the conceptual issues ought not to be obscured. The very admission of plural societies entails our depending on distinctions within the race; all such distinctions invite the charge of inequality, on some doctrinal grounds; not all such distinctions can be challenged nontendentiously; the elimination of determinate inequalities is itself justified by introducing or tolerating others; and nothing follows regarding unequal entitlement, benefit, compensation, and penalty, from the admission of objectively measurable differences among human populations, that vindicates one ideology rather than another. To give the vote to infants may be arbitrary, but to withhold it from those who fall below a certain annual income is not, in any plain sense, fair or unfair. The issue must be met dialectically in a context in which the relevant facts are already interpreted in accord with partisan views. Here, there simply is no evidence that alternative schemes of unequal treatment cannot be defended with comparable power.

Notes

1. The pathos of birth in this regard is the special concern of the existentialists, particularly Heidegger. See Martin Heidegger, *Being and Time,* trans. John Macquarrie and Edward Robinson (London: SCM Press, 1962); also, Jean-Paul Sartre, *Being and Nothingness,* trans. Hazel Barnes (New York; Philosophical Library, 1956).

2. R. M. Hare, *Freedom and Reason* (Oxford: Clarendon, 1963), pp. 12-13.

3. Although the principle of universalizability, *a fortiori,* the principles of justice and equality as here construed, is purely formal (a logical or "linguistic" truth), Hare inconsistently hedges about universalizability, holding, apparently in *morally* sensitive cases, that the question is not one of consistent usage but rather of whether we are "prepared" to universalize a particular commitment. See, for instance, R. M. Hare, *The Language of Morals* (Oxford: Clarendon, 1952), pp. 89-90. The difficulties of Hare's argument are summarized in Joseph Margolis, *Values and Conduct* (New York: Oxford University Press, 1971), Ch. 4. For another vacuous formulation about universalizability, see Henry Sidgwick, *The Methods of Ethics,* 7th ed. (London: Macmillan, 1907), pp. 209-379.

4. This touches on a subtle issue regarding classification and appraisal; see Margolis, *Values and Conduct,* Chs. 5-6.

5. The Declaration is conveniently reprinted in A. I. Melden, ed., *Human Rights* (Belmont: Wadsworth, 1970), which contains a number of related documents as well.

6. Reprinted in Melden, *Human Rights.*

7. See David Braybrooke, *Three Tests for Democracy: Personal Rights, Human Welfare, Collective Preference* (New York: Random House, 1968), Ch. 1. Also, Hugo Bedau, "Egalitarianism and the Idea of Equality," in J. Ronald Pennock and John W. Chapman, eds., *Equality* (Nomos IX) (New York: Atherton, 1967); and W.T. Blackstone, ed., *The Concept of Equality* (Minneapolis: Burgess, 1969).

8. H. L. A. Hart,"Are There Any Natural Rights?"*Philosophical Review* 64(1955): 175-91.

9. Ibid. Hart himself recognizes, in a footnote, the impossibility of freeing the determinate forms of freedom from ideological complication.

10. See Pennock and Chapman, *Equality*. On the implications of poverty and economic inequality, see Frances Fox Piven and Richard A. Howard, *Regulating the Poor: The Functions of Public Welfare* (New York: Pantheon, 1971); and Gunnar Myrdal, *The Challenge of World Poverty* (New York: Pantheon, 1970).

11. See Nicholas Rescher, *Distributive Justice* (Indianapolis: Bobbs-Merrill, 1966). Rescher is primarily concerned with the paradoxes of distributive justice. See also Kenneth Arrow, *Social Choice and Individual Value* (New York: Wiley 1951). Complications affecting democratic theory are discussed in Robert A. Dahl, *A Preface to Democratic Theory* (Chicago: University of Chicago Press,1955),and Braybrooke, *Three Tests for Democracy*.

12. The issue is extraordinarily muddled, though the narrow question of the methodological aspects of psychometric studies need not concern us here. We may, perhaps, merely note that the difference between *IQ achievement* (as manifested in tests) and *genotypic intelligence* is regularly confused in the literature. Our issue is a conceptual one, may be considered conditionally and in the context of analogues of intelligence obviously more open to comparative measurement than intelligence may be at the present time, for example, race- or sub-population-linked disease that may be dangerous to the health or survival of the country. The principal discussions of the IQ controversy include: A. R. Jensen, "How Much Can We Boost IQ and Scholastic Achievement?" *Harvard Educational Review* 39(1969): 1-123; R. J. Herrnstein, "I.Q.," *The Atlantic Monthly* 228(1971): 43-64; R. J. Herrnstein, *I.Q. in the Meritocracy* (Boston: Little, Brown, 1971); H. J. Eysenck, *The I. Q. Argument: Race, Intelligence and Education* (New York: Library Press, 1971); Arthur R. Jensen, *Educability and Group Differences* (New York: Harper and Row, 1973). For some specimens of critical exchange and reaction, see Ken Richardson and David Spears, ed., *Race and Intelligence* (Baltimore: Penguin, 1971); David Layzer, "Heritability Analyses of IQ Scores: Science or Numerology?" *Science* 183(1974): 1259-66; and Theodosius Dobzhansky, *Genetic Diversity and Human Equality* (New York: Basic Books, 1973). Bernard Williams has explored the controversy by way of considering a society that attaches great prestige to membership in a warrior class, requiring great physical strength; see "The Idea of Equality," in *Philosophy, Politics and Society*, ed. Peter Laslett and W. G. Runciman (Oxford: Blackwell, 1969); see also, Vernon L. Allen, ed., *Psychological Factors in Poverty* (Chicago: Markham, 1970).

13. There is a curious extension of the argument regarding human rights, in Peter Singer's review, "Animal Liberation," of Stanley and Roslind Godlovitch and John Harris, eds., *Animals, Men and Morals* (New York: Grove Press, 1971), *The New York Review of Books*, 5 April 1973, 17-21. On the basis of the capabilities of animals, Singer concludes that animals have rights and that, as a consequence, we must, morally, become vegetarians. But he fails to distinguish having rights from what is right or wrong to do, and he offers no general account of the nature of rights that meets the charges of vacuity advanced above. (More recently, Singer has dropped the emphasis on rights, preferring equality, but the issue remains the same.)

11

Waste

Cynicism insinuates that current quarrels about our ecological crises are faddist and will be replaced next year by another social game. That may well be, although the issues at stake belong, in principle, to the first appearance of man as well as to his last. What often happens when questions of waste, pollution, and ecological imbalance are raised is that the most fashionable and familiar concerns of the day skew the presentation of the problem in favor of some partial and passing vision. For instance, in the United States, the trade-off between the Alaskan oil pipeline and the threatened danger to the Alaskan wilderness poses a short-run dilemma that, at one and the same time, stalemates the most enlightened arguments for and against, and commits us to rather local choices. One can also imagine that when the pollution of the French Riviera reaches an utterly intolerable stage, when the Riviera is abandoned by its army of fashionable vacationers, the question of resisting the spread of pollution *there* will no longer be raised. The decline of topical interest in insecticides is similarly gratuitous.[1] A generation or so ago, the underlying questions had been asked, somewhat remotely, in the context of the death of the sun, the rupture of protective atmospheric belts, the collision of the earth and the moon, and the irreversibility of entropy; more practically, they were raised in the context of nuclear warfare, chain reactions, the wholesale destruction of fish life by undersea explosions, and radioactive fallout. None of these threats has ever been shown to be unfounded, but the world has tired of them in just the way in which suburban America has ceased to build bomb shelters. The truth is that it is entirely unclear what we mean by conservation, waste, pollution, or ecological balance. For instance, is the very existence of New York City ecologically indefensible? Must the automobile and the airplane be "rejected?" Is the human race "polluting" the earth with its own offspring?

Such questions appear both idiotic and profound: profound because they oblige us to consider some reasoned accord with nature; idiotic, because their resolution hints at the "sensible" elimination of man. The fact is that there is absolutely no way in which to scan physical nature or the biosphere or even the biological conditions of human life alone in order to provide the proper norms for directing and appraising the cultural forms of human life. Considerations of mere survival are hardly enough. The fantastic truth about human existence is that the population of the earth is increasing exponentially regardless of whatever ecological disorders we may have introduced. Apparently, in 1650, the world's population was about 0.5 billion (that is, 0.5 thousand million) and was growing at a rate of 0.3 percent a year. At that rate, the world's population would have doubled in about 250 years. By 1970, the population was 3.6 billion and increasing at a rate of 2.1 percent a year—that is, doubling every 33 years. It is expected that the world's population will be about 7 billion by the year 2000 and that, short of some unforeseen catastrophe affecting mortality rates, the population growth curve could not possibly level off before 2000.[2]

Now, if we ask ourselves the stunningly simple question, How many people ought we to allow on the earth and how ought they to live?, we begin to see the conceptual issues. Two critical considerations affecting any rational response, *assuming that we have a model for the appropriate quality of global life,* cannot but have the most radical implications for the distribution and use of political power. These are, quite simply, the lopsidedly unequal consumption of unequally distributed world energy by a relatively small fraction of the planet's population, and the gradual exhaustion, under that condition, of the world's nonrenewable natural resources. For instance, in 1967, the United States consumed 34.8 percent of the total world energy available, whereas Communist Asia, chiefly China, consumed 4.8 percent of the available energy; and yet, the United States had a population a little more than a quarter of that of Communist Asia.[3] Also, as of 1970, when known global reserves of natural gas were calculated to last, at the current rate of consumption, for 38 years (at an exponentially adjusted rate, for 22 years), the United States was consuming 63 percent of those reserves. Assuming five times the reserves, consumed at an exponentially increased rate linked to the average annual rate of growth, the supply would last no more than 49 years. Correspondingly, United States petroleum consumption accounted for 33 percent of the total supply, that, at current consumption rates, could last for no more than 31 years (at the adjusted rate, for 20 years) and, assuming five times the known reserves as before, would last no more than 50 years.[4] Of course, the dislocations are aggravated by the existing system of political states committed to national sovereignty and to property rights affecting their own resources and activities. Thus, the United States holds 25 percent of the known gas reserves and Saudi Arabia and Kuwait jointly hold 32 percent of the petroleum reserves.[5]

Obviously, there can be no rational resolution of the implied problems without a conception of the normative organization of total global life; and there simply is no plan for planetary reorganization that is at once politically realistic, acceptable to the principal competing ideologies, and demonstrably supported by moral norms and rules themselves not open to serious dispute. Equally obviously, admitting the intractability of ideological quarrels and the relative intractability of national interests, we can expect that we will approach the exhaustion of strategic, nonrenewable resources before we make effective progress on a rational plan, *any* rational plan, for the allocation and use of the resources of the world—a fact that must itself play a very substantial role in deciding what, under the circumstances, *is* a rational option to pursue.

The Club of Rome, for one, has formalized a realistic solution to the problems of growth of population and capital. On their calculations, "the basic behavior mode of the world system [that is, the model of all causal forces affecting population, capital, food, nonrenewable resources, and pollution] is exponential growth of population and capital, followed by collapse"; unlimited growth is impossible and our only rational choice lies between "natural" limits, exhaustion of resources, famine, or the like, and self-imposed limits. Self-imposed limits rationally require a causally linked equilibrium between births and deaths and a similar linkage between capital investment and depreciation; it also requires a minimizing of input and output along these two parameters and an adjustable ratio between the two in accord with society's values.[6] The model leaves two further questions unresolved—one not even mentioned. On the realistic assumption that the world will not move to implement the formal solution within an interval safe from "natural" collapse, what realistic alternatives are there to world cooperation and world collapse? No answer is forthcoming. The Club's report faces the second, extraordinarily difficult, question of determining "how long should the equilibrium state exist [that is, the state in accord with some formal solution]." If the interval were sufficiently short, then very nearly any societal organization would survive; and if it were extended for a very long period, then we should have to consider the problem of persuading an existing population to curtail its immediate benefits in order to preserve the world system for some future generation to consider in its own time.[7]

Here, two factors are decisive: first, man has never, in a sense to be specified, had "a place in nature" and so can never "return" to one; second, it is conceptually impossible to demonstrate what, objectively, ought to be the distribution of goods and services to the world's population, and so, in all likelihood, men cannot escape giving their allegiance to conflicting ideologies.

The first consideration bears directly on the evolution of man. We now know, reliably, that man evolved from certain proto-hominid creatures that lacked a developed cerebrum but possessed an otherwise human-like body and carriage and, even more significantly, exhibited elements of cultural development in the use of weapons and the implied appearance of a rudimentary hunting society. The more controversial versions of this thesis, for instance, the view that man descended from certain murderous apes (not merely from carnivores) or that the Zinjanthropus creature of Tanganyika was or was not a distinct genus, we may set aside.[8] The critical point is that, on all the evidence, the proto-cultural achievements of the hominids preceded and made possible the development of the distinctly human brain, the evolution of which depended on the distinctive mode of existence those creatures evolved. What this signifies is that man has always exploited physical nature to satisfy his culturally evolved objectives and the development of the brain and man's higher cultural achievements have merely facilitated and deepened this alien tendency. Elaborated sympathetically, this is obviously the alienation theme of the Existentialists.[9] More strenuously developed, it signifies that *there are, in principle, no natural norms derivable from the non-human world, or from the merely biological condition of the human animal, that could justifiably govern the direction and appraisal of human culture.* Even fossil creatures inferior to man must have had a rudimentary culture. The gifted animal stock that, culturally groomed, yielded human beings was itself the product of its pre-human cultural environment. Man himself has produced a great variety of animal and plant species whose very survival, like that of the commercial turkey, would be impossible in a natural environment unmanaged by cultural intrusions. But man is the supreme intruder both because his biological development is substantially dependent on the evolution of pre-human and human culture and because the prospects of his survival depend on his science and technology and political and social adaptiveness.

This is not to deny that there are laws of nature that bear directly on the survival and health of man, that set minimal and maximal limits to his exploiting and transforming the physical world, including his own body. But these constraints are just that, the limits of physical possibility compatible with an enormous variety of cultural alternatives. In this sense, the proposals of the Club of Rome or any other contemporary ecologists oscillate between projecting the *physical limits* of human life and *the limits of ideological preference* within such limits. The trouble is that the arguments for the one are remote from those for the other, remote for conceptual, not merely technological, reasons. The human being is an essentially cultural creature. He cannot, for instance, behave as such without a command of language; his own biology is adapted to the context of evolving cultures; and his history is the lengthening record of his cultural domestication of nature.

All that is now changing. We are faced with the double truth that man's stay on earth is limited at best, regardless of the care with which he uses the planet, and that his actual use of the planet has greatly accelerated the day of reckoning, at least as far as the maintenance of favored modes of life is concerned.[10] From this point of view, it appears to be physically impossible to escape ecological imbalance in the long run, because the demands of human life, indeed, the demands of life itself and even the requirements of a stable physical earth, are outweighed, on the physical evidence, by destructive forces that cannot be permanently arrested. In the short run, we are faced with an equivocation, for man's existence and dominance of physical nature constitute a permanent ecological imbalance, *if* we mean by "imbalance" the dependence of *any* sustained equilibrium affecting the forms of life on the cultural decisions of man himself. If we mean by "imbalance" the relative disorder of any equilibrium preferred by man, then the concept cannot but be ideologically captured.

The only interesting sense in which to speak of ecological balance is the sense in which *rules* for the ordering of human life can be derived from a study of the *laws* governing physical nature, including that portion of physical nature that is culturally organized; and the only sense in which that is possible is the sense in which such laws set minima and maxima for the exploitation of nature.[11] But, precisely, that is the sense in which we can derive *no* rules for the direction of human life beyond the purely formal considerations of coherence, consistency with the facts and physical possibility, congruence between means and ends, and the like.

Ecological imbalance is the analogue of the problem of personal illness, but it is only a metaphorical analogue. As with illness, we tend to elaborate the concept of imbalance equivocally, concerned as we are both with damage to prudentially decisive natural systems and to doctrinally preferred values.[12] The double theme is nowhere more poignantly pursued than in Rachel Carson's *Silent Spring*, for Carson is concerned with the "needless havoc" of destroying wildlife *and* with the imprudent use of insecticides that threaten our own purposes, whatever they may be. In fact, nearly all the literature on pollution is committed to a comparably dual objective and all of it is noticeably firm only where it addresses the minima and maxima of physical possibility and impending dangers to generically prudential objectives.[13] But there is little discussion of the meaning of pollution in terms of culturally preferred values and there is almost no effort to define the term itself.

One fairly instructive observation is offered by Barry Commoner:

> The environmental crisis tells us that there is something seriously wrong with the way in which human beings have occupied their habitat, the earth. The fault must lie not with nature, but with man. For no one has argued, to my knowledge, that the recent advent of pollutants on the earth is the result of some natural change independent of man . . . . In an ecological cycle no waste can accumulate because nothing is wasted. Thus, a living thing that is a natural part of an ecosystem cannot, by its own biological activities, degrade that ecosystem; an ecosystem is always stressed from without. Human beings, as animals, are no less tidy than other living organisms. They pollutants on the earth is the result of some natural change independent of man . . . . In an ecological cycle no waste can accumulate closed, cyclical network in which all other living things are held.[14]

Commoner's thesis, which in effect lurks behind all programs of ecological reform, supposes quite straightforwardly that there *is* a natural, biological order, some so-called "ecosystem," that man has the option of preserving and, preserving which, he produces no pollution and no waste. But what if one argued that the mere erection of a city like New York City threatens and finally eliminates *some* portion of a given ecosystem, namely, just that portion that the city replaces and that cannot be located elsewhere? Of course, when that happens and when the most generic prudential concerns are not adversely affected in the short run, we are inclined to think of waste and pollution in terms of possible damage to the ongoing life of that established city. It is quite impossible to speak, as Commoner does, of some global ecosystem formulated independently of human cultural interests, to which men may reconcile those interests. *Any ecosystem that concerns man presupposes the range of his culturally evolved values and interests, constrained only in terms of physical possibility.* An ecosystem centered on man's continued existence is simply an ideology viewed in terms of physical viability; hence, there is absolutely no way to judge human politics and morality by reference to the "neutral" norms of ecological concern, except in the minimal sense of considering physical possibilities. Every realistic ideology is, implicitly, an ecological preference.

The proper parallel to draw is that between ecological balance and homeostasis. Every surviving organism may, quite trivially, be said to be homeostatically organized.[15] The question regarding living organisms concerns *which* homeostatic pattern to prefer, not whether or not viable organisms are actually functioning homeostatically. Correspondingly, every surviving human society and, in fact, every surviving aggregate of animal and plant life may, quite trivially, be said to be ecologically balanced. Death is the limit of individual life; extinction, the limit of ecosystems. Illness is deviance from acceptable norms of health, within the natural limits of birth and death; waste and pollution, deviance from acceptable norms of ecological balance, within the natural limits of entropy and the like. Also, the price of continued existence may be reduced or altered vitality; and the price of continued balance may be the extinction of part of a given system. But the norms of health and ecological balance reflect a conjunction of prudential and ulterior interests that cannot possibly be extrapolated from attention merely to any and all causal regularities or to any and all limits of physical possibility.

From this point of view, *pollution* is the source of disadvantage to the ongoing prudential and deeper substantive interests of a human community, resulting from the human use of physical resources. The destruction of the marine life of Lake Erie, for instance, may be construed as a manifestation of pollution in terms of its having damaged a physical resource that human beings might otherwise exploit. Otherwise, we might be driven to speak of entropic pollution—the gradual disorganization of workable energy by the mere use of energy for any project whatsoever. *Waste* is the source of the depletion or unexploitability of a physical resource resulting from human activities, viewed in terms of projects that might otherwise have been pursued or judged worthy of such consideration. The pollution of Lake Erie, therefore, is a form of waste both in the sense that the lake's marine life is no longer available for human use and in the sense that the effluents dumped into the lake might themselves have served as a resource for other human projects. Otherwise, we might be driven to speak of entropic waste—the gradual and inexorable loss of workable energy for any project whatsoever.

These apparent quibbles are a good deal more significant than they at first appear. Why should a developing Latin American or Middle East country not hold (given the extremely small petroleum resources of the world and appraising the efficiency of their use, the number of automobiles engaged, the purposes served) that the enormous use of gasoline by American automobiles constitutes a serious form of waste? And why should New Zealand not hold (given the causal consequences of nuclear explosions) that France's testing its atom bomb in the Pacific islands constitutes a serious form of pollution? Seen thus, the finitude of nonrenewable natural resources and the relative and variable inaccessibility of all resources signify that one community's resource may well be another's waste and one community's cost, another's pollution. There is no way of specifying ecological imbalance, pollution, or waste independently of ideologically partisan preferences. *Any* scheme of human endeavor carried out on the scale that modern states are capable of cannot but be viewed by the partisans of other states in terms of wasting and polluting resources. This is why there can be no technological solution to the ecological problem: that problem is nothing but the problem of global politics again, viewed in terms of survival and comparative viability.[16]

Synchronically, the resolution of ecological quarrels is largely a function of converging political and economic interests among distinct communities, whether adjoining cities or world powers. The prospect of resolution is unrealistic, of course, because political states act to maximize supplies of energy favorable to themselves and to monopolize nonrenewable resources. To insist that such a policy is inherently imprudent or stupid or opportunistic or unfair, is, in effect, to impose an additional ideological constraint on the proper use of the global ecosystem. Here, a decisive difficulty confronts all theories about the defensible exploitation of the system, diachronically considered. The ultimate ecological question is, What share of the resources of the world ought we to leave for succeeding generations and what efforts ought we exert, for those generations, in order to recover potential resources from existing waste and pollution?

The issue is a version of what John Rawls has called "the problem of justice between generations."[17] Rawls' solution, probably the most sustained attempt in the recent literature, depends upon the assumption of an "original position," an idealized condition of man in terms of which a social contract may be rationally defended that embodies certain preferred principles of justice.[18] On Rawls' view, the original position is constrained by a "veil of ignorance," in that "the parties [to the contract] do not know to which generation they belong or, what comes to the same thing, the state of civilization of their society. They have no way of telling whether it is poor or relatively wealthy, largely agricultural or already industrialized, and so on."[19] The thesis, sensible enough, is to provide principles of justice impartial in every conceivable respect, for instance, regarding differences in temporal and spatial location, differences in resources, natural gifts, and the like.[20] But the point of the exercise is that, beginning with a theory of justice that "assume[s] as little as possible,"[21] one can elaborate reasonable adjustments in the theory as the veil of ignorance is gradually removed. Actual conditions, then, are to be analyzed in terms of their *approximation* to idealized conditions (the original position).

The argument is a sort of moral analogue of gravitational theory, where actual forces are analyzed as approximations to idealized systems of forces. The trouble is that the information pertinent to the resolution of the ecological problem, *a fortiori*, to actual moral and political problems, cannot be viewed convincingly in terms of approximation to the conditions of justice in the original position, even if those conditions were defensible for the original position itself—a matter that deserves to be reviewed. For example, Rawls' assumptions require that the original position be one of "moderate scarcity," which Hume took to provide the minimal context for rational debates about justice: "Natural and other resources are not so abundant that schemes of cooperation become superfluous, nor are conditions so harsh that fruitful ventures must inevitably break down . . . the circumstances of justice obtain whenever mutually disinterested persons put forward conflicting claims to the division of social advantages under conditions of moderate scarcity."[22] The severe limitation, however, of nonrenewable resources, their unequal scarcity and varying accessibility within the geographical boundaries of different national states, the effect of waste and pollution produced by one state on the marked scarcity of the resources of another, the effect of an exponentially increasing population on the scarcity of global resources, all tend to show that Rawls' assumption of a condition of moderate scarcity, *relatively unchanged regardless of which generation one is born into,* is an utterly unrealistic one, utterly incapable of supporting convincing extrapolations for conditions of mounting and increasingly severe scarcity.

There simply is no continuity, in principle, between conceptions of justice that assume the veil of ignorance and moderate scarcity and whatever conceptions are appropriate for actual conditions of serious scarcity and related factors of ecological imbalance; for, in denying moderate scarcity, we must also reject the veil of ignorance in order to appreciate the actual, limited resources we have, the way in which different policies actually affect their accessibility and supply, and the actual inequalities that exist in the use of those resources. It is simply impossible, from this viewpoint, to consider the requirements of justice as obtaining regardless of which generation one is born into or regardless of the ecological condition and resources of the world. In fact, Rawls requires that the initial contractual agreement, within the original condition, exhibit "unanimity in perpetuity."[23] But one has only to ask himself whether he could possibly decide questions about the distribution of goods and services in similar ways if he assumed moderate scarcity remaining relatively constant regardless of which generation he was born into and if he assumed the imminent exhaustion of nonrenewable resources and a population spiral threatening such a markedly increased scarcity of resources that the quality of life of future generations could not compare with that of favored sectors of the present generation, no matter how equitably goods and services were distributed.[24]

It is quite revealing, in this regard, that Rawls makes the following motivational assumption about the parties in the original position:

> The parties are thought of as representing continuing lines of claims, as being so to speak deputies for a kind of everlasting moral agent or institution. They need not take into account its entire life span in perpetuity, but their goodwill stretches over at least two generations. Thus representatives from periods adjacent in time have overlapping interests. For example, we may think of the parties as heads of families, and therefore as having a desire to further the welfare of their nearest descendants.[25]

Nevertheless, it is clear that the policies of the contracting parties cannot fail to be different under the assumed conditions of moderate scarcity and of ecological imbalance; in fact, the motivation postulated may come into conflict with the egoism Rawls also assumes to operate ("everyone is authorized to advance his aims as he pleases").[26] Also, since Rawls' account is admittedly a version of a contractarian thesis, it seems designed to provide an account of justice suitable to relatively independent national states. In fact, Rawls favorably mentions "the principle of self-determination, the right of a people to settle its own affairs without the intervention of foreign powers."[27] But, however reasonable it may be in the context of moderate scarcity *and* relatively equally accessible natural resources, the principle is a source of ecological imbalance under the conditions already sketched. Contractarian considerations suitable for plural and independent peoples cannot be meaningfully applied to the total population of the earth.[28]

The issue leads, quite naturally, to a deeper one. Rawls offers as a first approximation to the principles of justice he believes "would be chosen in the original position," the following:

> First: each person is to have an equal right to the most extensive basic liberty compatible with a similar liberty for others.
> Second: social and economic inequalities are to be arranged so that they are both (a) reasonably expected to be to everyone's advantage, and (b) attached to positions and offices open to all.[29]

The details regarding basic liberties and advantage are not important to develop here. But Rawls insists that "it is possible, at least theoretically, that by giving up some of their fundamental liberties men are sufficiently compensated by the resulting social and economic gains. The general conception of justice imposes no restrictions on what sort of inequalities are permissible; it only requires that everyone's position be improved."[30] He also holds that the principles of justice are to be put in "a serial or lexical order," that is, that "those earlier in the ordering have an absolute weight, so to speak, with respect to later ones, and hold without exception."[31] The ordering itself, on Rawls' view, is an original contractarian interpretation of the Kantian principle that men ought to be treated "not as means only but as ends in themselves."[32]

Two considerations are decisive here. For one, under conditions of increasingly serious scarcity and ecological imbalance, restricting the basic liberties of one generation in order to improve the resource advantages of succeeding generations cannot be defended on the basis of these lexically ordered principles of justice: the men of the first generation must be treated as means toward securing the interests of subsequent generations, not as ends. Second, even in the context of moderate scarcity, it is difficult to understand how the fulfillment of the first principle would be appraised independently of the inequalities tolerated by the second: in this sense, the principles cannot be lexically ordered at all. And, in the context of ecological imbalance, since the condition of inequalities tolerated by the second principle cannot be "reasonably expected to be to everyone's advantage," there is absolutely no way to demonstrate that any existing generation ought, rationally, to sacrifice its present advantages to the interests of generations as yet unborn. In fact, Rawls' motivational assumption regarding any generation's interest to provide for its immediate offspring is quite inadequate to accommodate the kind of long-term planning and constraint relevant to present problems of ecological imbalance: the sacrifices required are simply not those of a society considered synchronically or, more generously, a society with a short diachronic spread.

The heart of the matter is simply that the long-term conservation of essential nonrenewable resources, the provision of unequal advantages for selected sectors of an ongoing world population, the failure to eliminate ideological disagreements about what constitutes waste and pollution, the prospect of an exponentially increasing population affecting the fairness of favoring existing communities or larger and larger future populations, the impossibility of resolving ecological problems on the principle of national self-determination, all conspire to render any familiar principles of justice, including Rawls' new formulation, totally incompetent. Imagine, for instance, applying a utilitarian conception of justice to Rawls' original position: in that event, we should be bound to sacrifice everything for the welfare of the enormously larger populations of the future.

The truth, then, is that any attempted resolution of the developing crisis of ecological imbalance, more or less in the spirit of Rawls' proposals and the Western moral tradition, requires a global ideology of some sort: national, regional, ethnic, racial, and class distinctions must be subordinated to whatever is taken to be the interests of the people of the entire planet. But then, the required ideology would have to provide norms for an ongoing life exceeding one or two generations and conceived in terms of an indefinitely extended equilibrium in which decline is minimized. In that sense, the lives of every generation would be better construed as means to maintaining some ongoing ecological balance rather than as ends in themselves, in the traditional sense supporting egoism, individualism, the self-determination of nations and peoples, and the like. But this, of course, merely obliges us to concede that any workable and relevant principles of justice are as yet not forthcoming, are ideologically quite radical, and are not by any means the only rationally viable possibilities in the offing. The incredible pressures resulting from extending traditional notions of justice diachronically, under the developing conditions of ecological imbalance and scarcity, may yet catapult us into desperate conspiratorial wars (say, by the principal powers, who are themselves stalemated) designed to annihilate at a stroke "excessive" and "expendable" populations and to capture strategic resources so as to permit, *in the future*, a more manageable control of the "required" equilibria. Anticipating the failure of world parliaments, on what grounds could such an option be rationally rejected?

Notes

1. See Rachel Carson, *Silent Spring* (Boston: Houghton Mifflin, 1962), which mobilized the general American reader against DDT.

2. See the report of The Club of Rome, *The Limits to Growth*, by Donella H. Meadows et al., (New York: Universe Books, 1971), Ch. 1. See also Ansley J. Cole, "The History of the Human Population," *Scientific American* 231(1974): 41-51.

3. See *Man's Impact on the Global Environment, Report of the Study of Critical Environmental Problems* (SCEP), sponsored by the Massachusetts Institute of Technology (Cambridge: MIT Press, 1970) and *The Limits to Growth*.

4. See *The Limits to Growth*.

5. Ibid.

6. Ibid., Chs. 4-5.

7. The story of the Ik provides an interesting extreme specimen, here, of social possibilities not normally admitted. See Colin M. Turnbull, *The Mountain People* (New York: Simon and Schuster, 1972).

8. The account is interestingly provided by Robert Ardrey, *African Genesis* (New York: Athenaeum, 1961), Ch. 1, though Ardrey is often taken to be a partisan of the more sensational and less documented claims. See, particularly, Alexander Alland, Jr., *The Human Imperative* (New York: Columbia University Press, 1972). See also Raymond A. Dart, *Adventures with the Missing Link* (New York: Harper, 1959); "Cultural Status of the South African Man-apes," *Annual Report of the Smithsonian Institute*, 1955 (Washington: Government Printing Office, 1956); Louis S. B. Leakey, *Adam's Ancestors* (New York: Longmans, Green, 1935); W. E. LeGros Clark, *The Fossil Evidence for Human Evolution* (Chicago: University of Chicago Press, 1957); *History of the Primates* (London: British Museum, 1962).

9. See, for example, Karl Jaspers, *Man in the Modern Age*, trans. Eden and Cedar Paul (London: Routledge and Kegan Paul, 1951).

10. For instance, see S P R Charter, *Man on Earth* (New Grove, 1970), where the two themes are explored, allegedly within a humanistic framework—without, however, going beyond a rather vague paean favoring the powers of human creativity. The same

theme appears, more optimistically, in R. Buckminster Fuller, *Comprehensive Design Strategy* (Carbondale: University of Southern Illinois, 1967).

11. Cf. Garrett Hardin, *Exploring New Ethics for Survival: The Voyage of the Spaceship Beagle* (New York: Viking, 1972), especially "The Tragedy of the Commons." The problem of the relationship between rules (or norms) and laws is a profound one—affecting such disparate issues, for example, as the defense of the natural law doctrine and the defense of the rationalist thesis that natural languages embody linguistic universals—that is, universal rules for which the human infant is, in a sense, programmed. The latter thesis is most prominently associated with the work of Noam Chomsky; see *Language and Mind*, enlarged edition (New York: Harcourt Brace Jovanovitch, 1972). But it is unsupported on empirical grounds and no one, including Chomsky, has been able even to demonstrate methodological grounds on which it could be decisively supported. We simply have no conceptual basis for explicating what may be meant, say, by the genetic or any alternative coding of rules as opposed to the coding of physical dispositions—noting, always, that rules, by definition, are capable of being violated and that laws of nature set the limits of physical impossibility. See also Joseph Margolis, "Mastering a Natural Language: Rationalists versus Empiricists," *Diogenes*, No. 84(1973): 41-57. The issue is important because only a version of the rationalist thesis of the *natural coding of rules* could upset the conclusions to which we so far have been drawn. In this respect, it is quite suggestive that Chomsky, in his recent Russell Lectures, should have brought together, without a clear conceptual linkage, his views of the underlying nature of language and of the directions in which political efforts ought to be pursued; see *Problems of Knowledge and Freedom* (New York: Pantheon Books, 1971).

12. Compare Joseph Margolis, *Psychotherapy and Morality* (New York: Random House, 1966), on the concept of illness.

13. For instance see Barbara Ward and René Dubos, *Only One Earth* (New York: W. W. Norton, 1972); Allan Chase, *The Biological Imperatives* (New York: Holt, Rinehart and Winston, 1971); Hardin, *Exploring New Ethics for Survival;* Carson, *Silent Spring;* Barry Commoner, *The Closing Circle* (New York: Alfred A. Knopf, 1971); *Man's Impact on the Global Environment; The Limits to Growth;* Charter, *Man on Earth.*

14. Commoner, *The Closing Circle*, pp. 125-26.

15. See Walter B. Cannon, *The Wisdom of the Body*, revised (New York: W. W. Norton, 1939); see also René Dubos, *Mirage of Health* (New York: Harper and Row, 1959).

16. See Hardin, *Exploring New Ethics for Survival.*

17. John Rawls, *A Theory of Justice* (Cambridge: Harvard University Press, 1971),§ 44.

18. Ibid., § 11.

19. Ibid., p. 287; cf. also, § 24.

20. Ibid., § 45, 24.

21. Ibid., p. 129.

22. Ibid., pp. 127-28.

23. Ibid., p. 147.

24. For instance, see Ward and Dubos, *Only One Earth*, Pts. III-IV.

25. Rawls, *A Theory of Justice*, p. 128.

26. Ibid., p. 136.

27. Ibid., p. 378

28. See ibid., § 1.

29. Ibid., p. 60.

30. Ibid., p. 62.

31. Ibid., pp. 42-43; also, § 39. Rawls regards the principle as an approximation, it is true, but he defends it pretty stoutly; see ibid., p. 45 and § 82.

32. Ibid., pp. 179-83.

12

Epilogue

Our topics are negativities, that is, deprivations or limitations of life or of some condition preeminently valued by human beings. Though they form a mixed collection, they all bear decisively on the prudential concerns of men. At least statistically, human beings tend to act to preserve their lives, to minimize pain, to insure a measure of power favoring what they take to be their interests, to satisfy their desires. There is no clear sense in which the list may be made complete; so much depends on the historical careers of different societies. Nor is there a need to complete it; the entries are merely determinable, merely statistically prevalent. In fact, as in war and suicide, prudential objectives may be rationally set aside. So they are informative about human nature in the neutral sense that empirical evidence confirms their ubiquity. It could not be shown that men ought always or are always obliged to act in accord with such concerns. The plausibility of holding that the sacrifice of a life may, on occasion, be a distinct good, *a fortiori,* the sacrifice of any limited prudential interest, shows the difficulty of that thesis. And, unless we could demonstrate once and for all the "proper" functions of human nature, we should have to fall back to conceding that the coherent ways in which human beings manage to systematize their interests constitute the only accessible creeds they have.

Ideologies and creeds may be regarded as action-guiding rationalizations, viable insofar as they so function, in the sense that they provide schemata for directing and influencing the lives of aggregates of people, for appraising one's conduct and that of others, and for justifying such direction and such appraisal. Human beings must believe a great many things about the value of life and the ranking of alternative patterns of conduct to be able to make sustained sense of their daily lives. It may even be impossible to survive without such systematic convictions, since neither instinct nor imprinting can account for the stability of human societies. Men are, uniquely, culturally fashioned creatures: trained from infancy to behave as persons, essentially through the mastery of language and what that may entail, they are trained as well to favor some particular culture's vision and to view some creed or other as, within limits, adequate to direct their lives. The continuity of every society confirms this.

But because they bear directly on prudential interests, the negativities here considered and others that could be added must be addressed by every viable creed. The question remains whether we might deal with each negativity in a way that is not merely ideologically skewed. In principle, there appear to be only two conceivable strategies for doing so: one, by going beyond ideology to ideals, norms, principles, or rules of conduct demonstrably valid for human nature as such; the other, by restricting ourselves to the neutral conceptual features of the negativities discussed, that every ideology must cope with, in providing a viable direction for life itself. For instance, every complex society must appraise its commitments to war. But if collective entities alone wage war, the conceptual discovery that such entities are fictitious sets unavoidable constraints on any rationally supported creed concerned with war's justifiability. Similarly, if a society considers the defensibility of abortion, then it must concede the dialectical advantage of defining abortion as "ending an unwanted pregnancy" or as "taking the life of an innocent fetus."

If the first strategy is impossible, then any apparent attempt of that sort would merely be the expression of another ideology taking precedence over the one presumably tested. The second provides a certain measure of neutrality, in the sense in which, being ideologically engaged, it is important *for rational agents* to determine what conceptual limits each negativity imposes on *any* otherwise viable creed.

On any plausible view, morality bears on the human treatment of human beings. Since they tend, on the evidence, to occupy themselves prudentially, morality may be fairly construed as a systematic concern with the prudential interests of others. In that sense, no moral doctrine could possibly neglect to provide instruction regarding the negativities examined. But then, an asymmetry arises regarding our treatment of ourselves and others: as morally responsible agents, we cannot disregard the putative interests of others but, as in suicide and war, we can, rationally, decide whether and when to waive our own prudential interests. In fact, only if the first strategy could be satisfactorily fulfilled could neutral constraints on one's treatment *of oneself* be formulated, comparable in power to whatever may be imposed on our treatment of others, which is itself an important and neutral insight regarding the prospects of a rationally viable creed. If even that is denied, no prospect of objectivity remains.

Men cannot manage the complexities of personal and community relations without ideologies, because they are forever obliged to improvise in unforeseen encounters, to act spontaneously in ways congruent with the expectations and tolerance of a large number of other persons. Creeds are indispensable. But if so, the neutral analyses offered in the foregoing chapters are, however necessary they may be, utterly incapable of providing a viable basis for the reasoned direction of any life at all. In this sense, philosophy must yield to ideology. Still, if it is impossible to raise any viable creed to the level of a universally valid morality, then it is also the better part of valor to explore whatever objectively confirmable constraints our negativities impose on competing creeds addressed to rational and informed men. Curiously, we do this best in a piecemeal way. The positive direction of human life by reference to philosophical discoveries (so-called normative ethics) inevitably betrays its own normative loyalties; and the philosophical analysis of the terms and judgments of ethical discourse (so-called metaethics) inevitably risks its neutrality to whatever extent it draws substantive conclusions about justifiable conduct. Another, more limited enterprise has been pursued here, namely, the study of those minimal constraints, dialectically required or conceptually necessary, that every partisan adjustment to the negativities considered must, rationally, accommodate. There seems to be no sustained inquiry of this sort in the philosophical literature; in fact, it has no name. (What it comes to is the study of *rational minima.*)

An ideology is viable if and only if it is effectively action-guiding for a given community; the question of its persuasiveness is a causal question, not one of justification; and its justification will be seen in rather different ways depending on whether we believe that an "objective" morality can, in principle, be defended. Lacking a demonstrably valid morality, we fall back to the limits of every rational creed. In this sense, the constraints successively uncovered in the foregoing chapters constitute specimens of the best that any of us can provide in an effort to eliminate, from otherwise viable doctrines, unacceptable elements of arbitrariness, opportunism, irrelevance, incoherence, special pleading and the like. We find ourselves in the middle of things, shaped by the tenets we have learned in learning our mother tongue; as rational agents, we can do no better than temper the most attractive creeds by testing them against whatever minimal constraints intelligence can find no way of discarding. Obviously, we are more than cool critics: we are jealous advocates of competing visions. But then, our serious involvement in the world's affairs is insured by our partisanship; and our neutrality, by scrupulously testing our commitments. As partisans, we strengthen our tenets against those of others; as rational partisans, we advocate no policies that violate the constraints we uncover.

Ineluctably, we do more. But the world has already collected such a confusing lot of moral and political visions, so many pretended demonstrations of the "truth" about our obligations and "natural interests," that it is no longer convincing to expect a decisive new discovery. There is too much that counts against the prospect: for instance, the fact that the human animal is classifiable without regard to normative distinctions of any kind; or that human beings emerge only culturally; or that competing cultural norms are of interest only to creatures already culturally indoctrinated; or that causal and justificatory questions are logically of quite different sorts; or that man has no fixed nature in terms of which normative values could be discovered once and for all; or that there are indefinitely many coherent, plausible, and non-convergent ideologies.

The lesson is comparatively straightforward, if ironic. We cling to life with an animal intensity, but we understand it only as culturally trained creatures. The questions we raise, like the answers we supply, are qualified by the local creed. Reason collects our interests as well as the conceptual boundaries within which directions may be issued. In fact, we say we are rational, in the double sense that adherence to the prudential concerns of the race is *prima facie* rational and adherence to the canons of consistent and coherent discourse is beyond dispute.

But every positive engagement surpasses our rational constraints, and we work to imitate the intensity of animal commitment.

Criticism signifies the effort of men to be scrupulous in mid-career. But ideologies take over, for no life can be satisfactorily led by attending to minimal constraints. Thus seen, the objective of the race cannot possibly be to discover unitary, eternal truths somehow obscured by human quarrels, but only whatever minimal restrictions intelligence may impose on the contests of partisans. Life, then, reaches not for total justification but for as much as we can master; and human societies, not for a single policy but a single arena.

Index